HISTORY OF SPORTS

BASEBALL

BY JOHN F. GRABOWSKI

Lucent Books, Inc.
San Diego, California

Titles in The History of Sports Series include:
Baseball
Basketball
Football
Golf
Hockey
Soccer

Library of Congress Cataloging-in-Publication Data

Grabowski, John F.
     Baseball / by John F. Grabowski.
          p.   cm. — (History of sports)
     Includes bibliographical references and index.
     Summary: Discusses the origins and evolution of the game of
baseball, as well as memorable events and key personalities
in the game's history.
     ISBN 1-56006-677-6 (lib.: alk. paper)
     1. Baseball—United States—History—Juvenile literature.
[1. Baseball—History.] I. Title. II. Series.
GV863.A1 .G72   2001
796.357—dc21   00-008756

Copyright © 2001 by Lucent Books, Inc.
P.O. Box 289011, San Diego, CA 92198-9011
Printed in the U.S.A.

Contents

FOREWORD

MORE THAN MANY areas of human endeavor, sports give us the opportunity to see the possibilities in our physical selves. As participants, we all too quickly find limits in how fast we can run, how high we can jump, how far and straight we can hit a golf ball. But as spectators we can surpass those limits as we view the accomplishments of others and see how fast, how smooth, and how strong a human being can be. We marvel at the gravity-defying leaps of a Michael Jordan as he strains towards a basketball hoop or at the dribbling of a Mia Hamm as she eludes defenders on the soccer field. We shake our heads in disbelief at the talents of a young Tiger Woods hitting an approach shot to the green or the speed of a Carl Lewis as he appears to glide around an Olympic track.

These are what the sports media call "the oohs and ahhs" of sports—the stuff of highlight reels and *Sports Illustrated* covers. But to understand a sport only in the context of its most artistic modern athletes is shortsighted, for it does little justice to the accomplishments of the athlete *or* to the sport itself. Far more wise is to view a sport as a continuum—a constantly moving, evolving process. On this continuum are not only the superstars of today, but the people who first played the sport, who thought about rules and strategies that would make it more challenging to play as well as a delight to watch.

Lucent Books' series, *The History of Sports*, provides such a continuum. Each book explores the development of a sport, from its basic roots onwards, and tries to answer questions that a reader might wonder about. Who were its first players and what sorts of rules did the sport have then? What kinds of equipment were used in the beginning and what changes have taken place over the years?

Each title in *The History of Sports* also identifies key individuals in the sport's history—people whose leadership or skills have made a difference in the way the sport is played today. Included will be the easily recognized names, the Mia Hamms and the Sammy Sosas, the Wilt Chamberlains and the Wilma Rudolphs. But there are also the names of past greats, people like baseball's King Kelly, soccer's Sir Stanley Matthews, and basketball's Hank Luisetti—who may be less familiar today, but were as synonymous with their sports at one time as the "oohs and ahhs" players of today.

Finally, the series looks at the aspects of a sport that are particularly important in its current point on the continuum. Baseball today is better understood knowing about salary caps and union negotiators. One cannot truly know modern soccer without knowing about the specter of fan violence at matches. And learning about the role of instant replay is critical to a thorough understanding of today's professional football games. In viewing a sport as a continuum, the strides that have been made along the way are that much more admirable. It is a richer view, and one that shows how yesterday's limits have been surpassed— and how the limits of today are the possibilities of athletes in the future.

America's National Pastime

I**T IS DIFFICULT**, if not impossible, to explain the mystical hold that baseball has over millions of people across the United States. At first glance, this pastoral contest between two teams appears to lack everything that attracts the modern sports fan.

Football, for example, is the sport of choice for those looking for violence and mayhem. Every play finds three-hundred-pound men running into one another in hopes of separating the ballcarrier from the prized possession he cradles in his arms. The violence found in baseball is generally limited to the occasional "purpose" pitch which may strike a batter and cause opposing dugouts to empty. After much shoving and pushing, order is usually restored with no more damage than a bruised ego or two.

Basketball players are known for their athleticism. The modern game, played "above the rim," showcases the gravity-defying moves of Michael Jordan wannabes, who soar through the air before slamming the ball home through the hoop. Baseball, on the other hand, seems deceptively simple to play. The occasional double play turned by a graceful infield combination is probably the most athletic move seen on the diamond.

Speed is hockey's selling point. Known as "the fastest sport on earth," hockey's nonstop pace forces spectators to focus their attention on the puck at all times or risk missing an important shot put past the goaltender. Speed, too, is important in baseball. Runners steal bases, fielders chase after batted balls, and pitches are thrown at speeds approaching one hundred miles per hour. These bursts of speed, however, are separated by periods of inactivity when pitchers hold on to the ball and batters step into and out of the batter's box as if afraid of the consequences of their next move.

Why, then, does baseball continue to retain its title as America's national pastime? Why is it, as writer and historian Jacques Barzun once wrote, that "Whoever wants to know the heart and mind of America had better learn baseball?"[1]

The answer, perhaps, can be found in the game's long, rich history. This history—more than that of any other major team sport—reflects the story of life in America. Race relations, patterns of im-

migration, the struggle between labor and management—all can be found mirrored in the annals of baseball.

No other sport has been analyzed as much as baseball. For more than a century, the stories of individual games have been recorded in box scores which enable events to be re-created, oftentimes pitch by pitch, years later. The numbers associated with the game and its players have been crunched in every conceivable way by fans and researchers alike. These analyses allow the Tony Gwynns and Randy Johnsons of today to be compared to the Ty Cobbs and Cy Youngs of yesteryear. The question, "Who was the greater home-run hitter, Babe Ruth or Mark McGwire?" will undoubtedly continue to be argued throughout the new millennium.

The legends of yesteryear are often compared with current stars such as pitcher Randy Johnson (pictured).

Baseball is a simple game. According to writer H. J. Dutiel, it consists of "tapping a ball with a piece of wood, then running like a lunatic."[2] It is played by most American boys and many American girls at some time in their lives. It is played in all parts of the country, by young and old, rich and poor, black and white. At its highest levels, it is played by more average-sized people than either football or basketball. It is easier, therefore, for youngsters to identify with baseball players than with athletes in other sports. Regardless of a person's position in life, there seem to be few handicaps which cannot be overcome in the drive to achieve success on the ball field. After all, Babe Ruth, arguably the greatest player ever, spent the formative years of his life being raised in what was basically a reform school.

The game of baseball is timeless. It is the only major team sport in which play is not controlled by a clock. An inning's duration may be five minutes or an hour and five minutes. If the score is tied after nine innings, the game continues until one team emerges victorious. There is no "shoot-out" or coin toss to give one side an overtime advantage. Each team has an equal number of turns at bat and an equal number of outs. "Since baseball time is measured only in outs," wrote Roger Angell, "all you have to do is succeed utterly; keep hitting, keep the rally alive, and you have defeated time. You remain forever young."[3]

Although each of these explanations may be responsible, in part, for baseball's popularity, none is adequate to explain it fully. There still remains a unique attraction which cannot be measured or quantified. In his book *Ball Four*, former major-league pitcher Jim Bouton wrote, "You spend a good piece of your life gripping a baseball and in the end it turns out that it was the other way around all the time."[4] Perhaps that says it best of all.

CHAPTER 1

From Across the Ocean

NO OTHER GAME captures the essence of our country's character as does baseball. It might seem only natural, then, that the origin of this American pastime be purely American. The truth, however, is a different story.

The Doubleday Myth

In 1889, a troupe of ballplayers sailed into New York harbor after having completed a celebrated world tour. The tour had been organized by former pitcher Albert G. Spalding. Its stated purpose was to popularize the game of baseball overseas. In doing so, it also created new markets for equipment, which would be supplied, co-incidentally, by the A. G. Spalding & Bros. sporting goods company.

The returning players were honored at a banquet hosted by National League president A. G. Mills. During the course of the evening, Mills rose to speak. In a burst of patriotism, he professed the view that baseball was entirely of American origin, not, as rumor had it, an amusement derived from the English game of rounders. Spalding, along with the others in attendance, applauded Mills's proclamation.

One of the main proponents of the rounders theory was baseball's most well versed historian, Henry Chadwick, the editor of *Spalding's Official Base Ball Guide*. The ongoing debate between Chadwick and his boss eventually caused Spalding to call for the formation of a seven-man commission to research the matter. A. G. Mills was named chairman of the board, whose members were handpicked by Spalding. In 1907, the commission arrived at the surprising conclusion that a single man—Civil War general Abner Doubleday—originated the sport of baseball in Cooperstown, New York, in 1839. This conclusion was based solely on a letter the commission received from an elderly Cooperstown native by the name of Abner Graves. Graves claimed to have been in attendance on the day sixty-eight years earlier when Doubleday laid down the rules for his invention.

Spalding happily accepted the commission's report. "It certainly appeals to an American's pride," he wrote, "to have had

Albert G. Spalding, who worked to popularize the game of baseball.

the great national game of Base Ball created and named by a Major General in the United States Army."[5]

The only problem with the conclusion was that it was extremely unlikely. In 1839, Abner Doubleday was a first-year student at the U.S. Military Academy in West Point. Ineligible for leave, he spent no time in Cooperstown that year. In addition, the general, who died in 1893, left behind numerous diaries. None contained any claims to having invented the game of baseball. In fact, Mills himself had known Doubleday personally during the war and could not recall him ever mentioning having a part in the sport's birth.

A more likely explanation of Graves's recollections was unearthed years later. Apparently, there indeed was an Abner Doubleday living in Cooperstown in 1839, but this was the general's cousin. That young man undoubtedly played the game of town ball, which was a forerunner of the modern game of baseball popular during that period.

In spite of the evidence to the contrary, a public eager to hear what it wanted accepted the commission's findings. The Doubleday myth stood without further challenge until 1939, when a more reasonable explanation of the game's evolution was demonstrated.

English Roots

Bat-and-ball games have been played by mankind for centuries. The east wall of

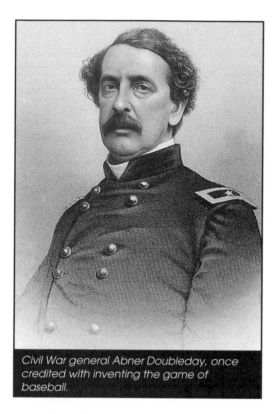

Civil War general Abner Doubleday, once credited with inventing the game of baseball.

the Shrine of Hathor at the Temple of Deir-er-Bahari in Egypt is adorned with a thirty-five-hundred-year-old painting of the pharaoh Thothmes III hitting balls to two priests.

In fifteenth century England, youngsters often played games of ball to celebrate religious holidays. One of the most popular of these was known as stoolball. In its simplest form, the game was played by two persons, one of whom stood in front of a small stool. The thrower would stand across from him and try to toss the ball past the first player so that it would hit the stool. The hitter would try to swat

the ball with his hand. They kept track of the number of times the ball was hit. If the thrown ball hit the stool, the players switched places. When other players joined in, other stools were added. Players ran from one post to another on hit balls, while fielders tried to "put out" the hitter by throwing the ball at him.

Eventually, this primitive game evolved into two more advanced pastimes—cricket and a game sometimes referred to as baseball. Both sports have been played in Britain for several centuries.

Cricket

Cricket is the more formalized of the two sports and bears the closest resemblance to stoolball. Played on a large field called a pitch, most of the action in cricket takes place in the central area, where two three-legged wickets stand some twenty-two yards apart. These wickets bear a striking resemblance to the stools used in stool-ball, stools which were at one time, in fact, called crickets. The wickets are wooden structures consisting of three poles, across which are placed two long pieces of wood called bails.

The batsman stands at one end of the pitch, defending the wicket, while the pitcher, or bowler, stands at the other end. Another batsman also stands at the bowler's end. The bowler attempts to put out the batsman by hurling the ball past him, and breaking his wicket. The batsman protects his wicket by swinging at the ball with a flat-sided bat, or blade. He tries to hit the ball so that he and his partner can score, which they do by exchanging places without either wicket being broken. The defensive fielders are stationed at various parts of the field. They can put out the batsman by catching a hit ball on the fly or by throwing him out. To do this, the fielder must hit the wicket with a thrown ball before a runner reaches it safely.

A regulation cricket match consists of either one or two innings. An innings (the word is both singular and plural) consists of the time it takes each member of the eleven-member team to bat until he is retired, or his "wicket is taken." Since the batter does not have to swing at a pitch if he does not think he can reach the next wicket safely—or even run if he does hit it—a single match can sometimes take days to complete.

Rounders

The other offshoot of stoolball had many variations, the most common being the game known as rounders. The modern version of rounders is played on a five-sided field, with posts located at four of the corners serving as bases. The batter stands at the batting square in the fifth corner. The bowler throws the ball from the bowling square in the center of the field, and the batter swings at it with a short bat held in one hand. After hitting the ball, the batter and runners take off for the next base. If they touch the post with either their hand or bat, they cannot be put out. A runner who

Cricket, a game that bears a close resemblance to an earlier game called stoolball, has been played in Britain for several centuries.

reaches the fourth post safely scores a "rounder." An innings is the time it takes for every member of the nine-member team to bat until he is put out. The team with the most runs scored after two innings is the winner.

British soldiers brought both cricket and rounders with them to the colonies in the eighteenth century. Rounders, the more popular of the two games, soon mutated into two variations—town ball, or the Massachusetts game, and baseball, known as the New York game.

The Massachusetts Game

Town ball was popular throughout the New England region, as well as in New York and Pennsylvania. The bases were stakes, as in rounders, but the shape of the field was square rather than pentagonal. The "thrower" stood in the middle of the field and pitched the ball to the "striker," who stood halfway between "first stake" and "home stake." The batter was put out if he swung at—and missed—three pitches, or if he hit a ball which a fielder caught on the fly. A runner could be put out if he was "plugged" by a thrown ball. Each inning consisted of just a single out, and games were played until one team reached one hundred scores, or tallies.

The rules of this game were eventually formalized by the Massachusetts Association of Base Ball Players in 1858. The very next year saw the first intercollegiate ball game played between teams from Amherst

College and Williams College. Amherst came out on top, besting Williams by a score of 73–32.

In the meantime, town ball was facing stiff competition from another variation of the game which was increasing in popularity in the New York City vicinity. This pastime, known as the New York game, would develop into the game of baseball known today.

Alexander Cartwright and the New York Game

In the early 1840s, town ball and its variations were enjoyed as a form of exercise by young Manhattan clerks, storekeepers, and middle-class businessmen. On September 23, 1845, a group of them from the Madison Square and Murray Hill sections of the city banded together to form a fraternal organization called the Knickerbocker Base Ball Club. A twenty-five-year-old bank teller named Alexander Joy Cartwright is acknowledged as being the organizer of the group. He is also credited with being one of the persons responsible for setting down the first set of rules for the game, often referred to as the "Cartwright rules."

In this game, the field was laid out in the shape of a diamond, with the batter standing at one of the corners. The pitcher threw from a "pitcher's box" located in the center of the diamond. Bases, not posts, marked each of the corners. The distance between bases was set at ninety feet. Only balls hit between the first- and third-baselines were considered to be in play, making the New York game the first to restrict the playing field. Balls hit by the batter could be caught on the fly, or on a single bounce, for an out. The practice of putting a runner out by "plugging" or "soaking" him with the ball was not allowed. Games were played until a score of twenty-one runs, or "aces," was reached, but a game of nine innings in length soon became standard. Nine players per side also became the norm.

With the stretch between bases a more "adult" distance, and the childish practice of "plugging" the runner with a thrown ball no longer permitted, the game had a stronger appeal to the adult population than did town ball. Although Cartwright's role in the invention of baseball is open to debate, he is still recognized as the father of modern baseball. He was elected to the Baseball Hall of Fame in 1938, where his plaque at Cooperstown reads:

ALEXANDER JOY CARTWRIGHT, JR.
"FATHER OF MODERN BASEBALL"
SET BASES 90 FEET APART.
ESTABLISHED 9 INNINGS AS GAME
AND 9 PLAYERS AS TEAM. ORGANIZED
THE KNICKERBOCKER BASEBALL CLUB
OF N.Y. IN 1845. CARRIED BASEBALL
TO PACIFIC COAST AND HAWAII
IN PIONEER DAYS.[6]

Although there is evidence that other teams were active prior to the formation of the Knickerbockers, it is generally accepted that Cartwright's club was the first to have a regular organization, as opposed to simply being an informal gathering of players. On June 19, 1846, twenty-eight members of the club took the ferry across the river to Hoboken, New Jersey. There, at the Elysian Fields, they played the first officially recorded game between two teams under the Cartwright rules. Although Cartwright himself did not play, he umpired the contest, which saw the New York Ball Club defeat the Knickerbockers by a score of 23–1 in four innings.

The game, basically, was a social event among friends. It is important to understand that these were clubs and not teams. A club was a social as well as an athletic association. In the beginning, at least, the social functions were more meaningful than the athletic. These functions might include gatherings such as suppers and formal balls. A ball game often simply served as a preamble to the meal which followed.

The young men who made up the clubs were more interested in playing the game for recreation and exercise than they were in competition. Most games in these years, in fact, were essentially contests among members of the same club rather than interclub matches. In time, rival clubs began imitating the Knickerbockers, and Cartwright's rules began to gain acceptance.

The National Association

Baseball's popularity boomed in the 1850s. In 1858, several of the New York area clubs banded together to form the first baseball organization—the National Association of Base Ball Players. By the onset of the Civil War, baseball had surpassed town ball as the game of choice. Although cricket still had many followers, Union soldiers helped the spread of baseball by playing it throughout the South. By the end of the war, interest in the game was at an all-time high. The *New York Herald* confidently stated that "the national game of America is now *par excellence,* baseball."[7]

The attitude toward playing the game began to change as its popularity increased. Winning became more important than simply playing for the fun of it. Clubs, however, continued to be clubs rather than teams. Some had as many as four hundred or more members. Only the best players performed with the first team; others might play for the club's "muffins," or lower teams, or simply cheer on their fellow members.

As it became clear that there was interest in viewing these contests, entrepreneurs came to see the possibilities for making a profit. In 1862, William Cammeyer, who owned the land on which the Brooklyn Union Club played, enclosed the field. On May 15, the Union Baseball Grounds opened for the first time, with Cammeyer charging an admission fee of ten cents per person to watch the game. Other businessmen soon followed suit. Clubs began insisting on a portion of the profits, as did some of the players. The problems this presented were obvious. Games could be arranged to be won or lost in hopes of increasing interest and attendance at the next meeting between the teams. With additional sums of money being wagered on the outcomes of games by spectators in the audience, a further enticement to tampering was introduced.

The Beginning of Professionalism

Although the National Association insisted that players not be paid salaries, by the late 1860s, many, in fact, were. Some clubs gave players money under the table, while others paid salaries for imaginary jobs.

On September 9, 1868, the Cincinnati Base Ball Club became the first team to publicly announce that it was going to pay its players for playing ball. (At its meeting three months later, the National Association agreed to recognize professional players for the first time.) Club president Aaron B. Champion hired well-known cricket player Harry Wright to put his new professional team together. As captain and manager, Wright assembled some of the best players of his time, including himself and his brother, George. Players were paid stipends ranging from six hundred to fourteen hundred dollars. Such salaries were

TOWN BALL RULES

The following are "The Rules & Regulations Governing The Game Of Base Ball As Adopted By The Massachusetts Association Of Base Ball Players At Dedham, May 13, 1858," as printed in "The Base Ball Player's Pocket Companion" in 1859. They are here reprinted from *The Old Ball Game* by Mark Alvarez.

1. The Ball must weigh not less than two, nor more than two and three-quarter ounces, avoirdupois. It must measure not less than six and a half, nor more than eight and a half inches in circumference, and must be covered with leather.

2. The Bat must be round, and must not exceed two and a half inches in diameter in the thickest part. It must be made of wood, and may be of any length to suit the Striker.

3. Four Bases or Bounds shall constitute a round; the distance from each Base shall be sixty feet.

4. The Bases shall be wooden stakes, projecting four feet from the ground.

5. The Striker shall stand inside of a space of four feet in diameter, at equal distance between the first and fourth Bases.

6. The Thrower shall stand thirty-five feet from and on a parallel line with the Striker.

7. The Catcher shall not enter within the space occupied by the Striker, and must remain upon his feet in all cases while catching the Ball.

8. The Ball must be thrown—not pitched or tossed—to the Bat, on the side preferred by the Striker, and within reach of his Bat.

9. The Ball must be caught flying in all cases.

10. Players must take their knocks in the order in which they are numbered; and after the first innings is played, the turn will commence with the player succeeding the one who lost on the previous innings.

11. The Ball being struck at three times and missed, and caught each time by a player on the opposite side, the Striker shall be considered out. Or, if the Ball be ticked or knocked, and caught on the opposite side, the Striker shall be considered out. But if the Ball is not caught after being struck at three times, it shall be considered a knock, and the Striker obliged to run.

12. Should the Striker stand at the Bat without striking at good Balls thrown repeatedly at him, for the apparent purpose of delaying the game, or of giving advantage to players, the referees, after warning him, shall call one strike, and if he persists in such action, two and three strikes; when three strikes are called, he shall be subject to the same rules as if he struck at three fair Balls.

13. A player, having possession of the first Base, when the ball is struck by the succeeding player, must vacate the Base, even at the risk of being put out; and when two players get on one Base, either by accident or otherwise, the player who arrived last is entitled to the base.

14. If a player, while running the Bases, be hit with the Ball thrown by one of the opposite side, before he has touched the home bound, while off a Base, he shall be considered out.

15. A player, after running the four Bases, on making the home bound, shall be entitled to one tally.

16. In playing all match games, when one is out, the side shall be considered out.

17. In playing all match games, one hundred tallies shall constitute the game, the making of which by either Club, that Club shall be judged the winner.

18. Not less than ten nor more than fourteen players from each Club, shall constitute a match in all games.

19. A person engaged on either side, shall not withdraw during the progress of the match, unless he be disabled, or by the consent of the opposite party.

20. The referees shall be chosen as follows: One from each Club, who shall agree upon a third man from some Club belonging to this Association, if possible. Their decision shall be final, and binding upon both parties.

21. The tallymen shall be chosen in the same manner as the referees.

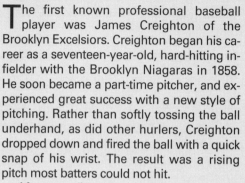

JAMES CREIGHTON, BASEBALL'S FIRST SUPERSTAR

The first known professional baseball player was James Creighton of the Brooklyn Excelsiors. Creighton began his career as a seventeen-year-old, hard-hitting infielder with the Brooklyn Niagaras in 1858. He soon became a part-time pitcher, and experienced great success with a new style of pitching. Rather than softly tossing the ball underhand, as did other hurlers, Creighton dropped down and fired the ball with a quick snap of his wrist. The result was a rising pitch most batters could not hit.

After spending part of 1859 with the Niagara Stars, Creighton jumped to the Brooklyn Excelsiors the next season. He became the team's ace pitcher, while continuing to excel as a hitter. Incredibly, some baseball historians credit him with having played an entire season without being put out a single time.

When he was not pitching, Creighton continued to play both the infield and outfield. He was an above-average fielder who is credited with starting what may well have been the first triple play ever. It occurred during a game between the Brooklyn Excelsiors and the Baltimore Excelsiors on July 22, 1860.

Creighton's abilities on the field were enough to make him one of the early legends of the game, and his tragic death insured that he would never be forgotten. While playing against the Unions of Morrisania on October 14, 1862, the young slugger took a mighty swing at a pitch. A loud pop could be heard by the catcher and on-deck hitter, and the ball sailed toward the outfield. After rounding the bases and crossing the plate with a home run, Creighton told a teammate that he must have snapped his belt. The truth, however, was far more serious: the young star had ruptured his bladder. Creighton passed out on the field and was rushed to his father's house. After clinging to life for several days, Creighton finally passed away from internal hemorrhaging on October 18, at the age of twenty-one.

not to be dismissed lightly. The average common laborer of the day earned less than five hundred dollars per year, while skilled craftsmen might expect to take home eight hundred dollars annually.

Wright's talent for organization made his team an immediate success. The Red Stockings, as they were known, practiced harder and longer than other teams. Plays, such as cutoffs, were repeated countless times until they became a matter of habit to the players. In order to put as much time as they did into preparation, the players had to be in excellent condition. Wright's training methods saw to it that his players were in the best physical shape possible. His total devotion to the game was noted by the Cincinnati *Enquirer*: "[Harry Wright] eats base-ball, breathes base-ball, thinks base-ball, dreams base-ball, and incorporates base-ball in his prayers."[8]

The Red Stockings opened the 1869 season with several easy victories over local teams. They proceeded to take their game on the road, barnstorming from coast to coast against the top teams. Their reputation grew by leaps and bounds as team after team went down in defeat. Fans came out in unheard-of numbers to see the Cincinnati juggernaut.

By the time the season was over, the Red Stockings had won every one of their fifty-seven matches against other clubs. Their dominance was illustrated by their 42–10 average margin of victory. More than two hundred thousand fans turned out to see them play that year, but financially the result was less than successful. The team's share of the gate receipts came out to $29,726.26, but their expenses totaled $29,724.87. Their payoff was a grand profit of $1.39.

The beginning of the 1870 season saw Cincinnati continue its winning ways. The team won its first twenty-seven games before finally losing an 8–7, eleven-inning thriller to the Brooklyn Atlantics on June 14. The loss ended the Red Stockings's

amazing winning streak at eighty-four consecutive games. The team's success, on the field and at the gate, insured that professional baseball was here to stay. At least four other professional teams were operating by the end of 1870. It seemed only a matter of time before these pro teams would form their own organization.

The National Association of Professional Base Ball Players

The first professional league—the National Association of Professional Base Ball Players—came into existence on March 17, 1871. The nine teams which entered into the union were the Philadelphia Athletics, Boston Red Stockings, Chicago White Stockings, Cleveland Forest Cities,

The Cincinnati Red Stockings dominated their league in 1869 and 1870, paving the way for other professional teams.

HENRY CHADWICK, CONSCIENCE OF THE GAME

The only writer ever elected to the Baseball Hall of Fame proper (as opposed to the Writers Wing) was a distinguished-looking gentleman by the name of Henry Chadwick. Born in England, Chadwick came to the United States as a young boy in 1837. He played rounders as a youngster, but in time came to be fascinated by the emerging sport of baseball. He took it upon himself to spread the gospel of the game both far and wide. As a reporter, he covered baseball regularly for several New York newspapers, including the *Times, Tribune,* and *Herald.* He later edited *Beadle's Dime Base Ball Player,* the sport's first annual guide, and *Spalding's Guide* from 1881 to his death in 1908. Chadwick devised a detailed system of scoring games, which led him to produce the forerunner of the modern-day box score and the game's first detailed statistics.

Chadwick also had a hand in shaping baseball's development. For years he was a member of the official rules committees. He did not hesitate to voice his opinion on matters he considered vital to the game, railing against ungentlemanly conduct, drinking, and gambling. For his many contributions, Chadwick came to be known as the "Father of Baseball," and oftentimes was simply called "Father Chadwick."

Rockford Forest Cities, Troy Haymakers, Washington Olympics, New York Mutuals, and Ft. Wayne Kekiongas (who later quit and were replaced by the Brooklyn Eckfords).

Problems besieged the new league from its very first year. The Great Chicago Fire destroyed the White Stockings's ballpark, forcing the team to play out its season on the road while using borrowed equipment. Fan interest dropped significantly in 1872 when the Boston Red Stockings, led by George Wright and Al Spalding, began to run away from the competition. Some teams dropped out of the league due to lack of fan support, while others failed to play out their schedules. Fans who did attend games became rowdier and harder to control. Gambling was rampant, and rumors of fixed contests abounded. Additional problems involving corruption and team and player instability further weakened the National Association and its perception in the public eye.

After five seasons, it became obvious that the National Association was not the answer. A stronger central authority was needed to police professional baseball. That void would be filled by the National League of Professional Base Ball Clubs in 1876.

CHAPTER 2

The Field of Play

BASEBALL'S MAIN COMPETITION in the mid–1800s was from town ball, or the Massachusetts game. Part of the reason for baseball's eventual ascension was that town ball did not have an official set of rules until those adopted by the Massachusetts Association of Base Ball Players in 1858. By that time, Cartwright's Knickerbocker Rules had already been in existence for over a decade.

The Knickerbocker Rules of 1845

Listed below are the twenty rules of the Knickerbocker Base Ball Club, as adopted on September 23, 1845:

1. Members must strictly observe the time agreed upon for exercise, and be punctual in their attendance.

2. When assembled for exercise, the President, or in his absence the Vice-President, shall appoint an Umpire, who shall keep the game in a book provided for that purpose, and note all violations of the By-Laws and Rules during the time of exercise.

3. The presiding officer shall designate two members as Captains, who shall retire and make the match to be played, observing at the same time that the players put opposite to each other should be as nearly equal as possible; the choice of sides to be then tossed for, and the first in hand to be decided in like manner.

4. The bases shall be from "home" to

21

second base, forty-two paces; from first to third base, forty-two paces, equidistant.

5. No stump match shall be played on a regular day of exercise.

6. If there should not be a sufficient number of members of the Club present at the time agreed upon to commence exercise, gentlemen not members may be chosen in to make up the match, which shall not be broken up to take in members that may afterwards appear; but, in all cases, members shall have the preference, when present, at the making of a match.

7. If members appear after the game is commenced they may be chosen in if mutually agreed upon.

8. The game to consist of twenty-one counts, or aces; but at the conclusion an equal number of hands must be played.

9. The ball must be pitched, and not thrown, for the bat.

10. A ball knocked out of the field, or outside the range of the first or third base, is foul.

11. Three balls being struck at and missed and the last one caught, is a hand out; if not caught is considered fair, and the striker bound to run.

12. If a ball be struck, or tipped, and caught, either flying or on the first bound, it is a hand out.

13. A player running the bases shall be out, if the ball is in the hands of an adversary on the base, or the runner is touched with it before he makes his base; it being understood, however, that in no instance is a ball to be thrown at him.

14. A player running who shall prevent an adversary from catching or getting the ball before making his base, is a hand out.

15. Three hands out, all out.

16. Players must take their strike in regular turn.

17. All disputes and differences relative to the game, to be decided by the Umpire, from which there is no appeal.

18. No ace or base can be made on a foul strike.

19. A runner cannot be put out in making one base, when a balk is made by the pitcher.

20. But one base allowed when a ball bounds out of the field when struck.[9]

The Knickerbocker Rules gave baseball an appeal that was lacking in other games of the day. With home plate and second base—and first base to third—laid out forty-two paces apart, the distance between one base and the next came close to the current ninety feet. This was a more "adult" distance than the sixty feet or less between bases common in other games.

Likewise, the senseless method of recording an out by "plugging" a runner with a thrown ball was eliminated. Tagging a runner, or base, in order to register an out led to a more scientific approach to the game. Positioning and teamwork played a more important role. Doing away with plugging had an additional benefit, since a harder ball could be used. The ball could be hit more sharply and thrown more accurately, resulting in crisper movements on the field, which required more finely honed skills.

The Knickerbocker Rules also made the game more attractive to spectators. The baselines set down by Cartwright created an area of foul territory which was out of play. This insured that spectators could get closer to the action than in sports such as cricket, rounders, or town ball.

Another factor which added to baseball's growing popularity was the time it took to complete a game. A game of town ball, played to a score of one hundred, could drag on for hours on end, while a cricket match often lasted more than a single day. A game of baseball, however, played to a score of twenty-one "aces," usually was over within a couple of hours. (The rule limiting a regulation game to nine innings

As a result of Alexander Cartwright's creation of foul territory, spectators can get closer to baseball action.

of play was not adopted until 1857. This further reduced the number of long, drawn-out contests.)

Although most features of the Knickerbocker game would be recognizable to modern-day fans, others would not. The umpire, for example, did not stand on the field or affect the play of the game. Instead, he sat at a table along one of the baselines, only making a decision if a dispute arose. He would occasionally ask for the opinion of nearby spectators if he was not sure of a ruling. It was assumed, of course, that the spectators would be impartial in their judgments.

Another rule called for the pitch to be tossed to the batter underhand, and delivered with a straight elbow and wrist. Rather than trying to deceive the batter, the "feeder's" job was to give him a pitch he could hit. Since no balls or strikes were called, the batter could wait indefinitely until he got a pitch to his liking. Since that time, a good number of the most significant changes the game has seen have been those affecting the delicate balance between pitching and hitting.

Called Balls and Strikes

When the National Association of Base Ball Players was formed in 1858, representatives of the twenty-five member clubs refined and expanded the Knickerbocker Rules. The size of the ball and bat were specified in more exact terms, as was the distance between bases. Perhaps the most important rule change dealt with the role of the umpire.

Prior to this time, the pitcher tried to toss the ball so that the batter could hit it. There were no penalties for pitchers who consistently threw outside of the area preferred by the batter. Likewise, there were no penalties for batters who were exceedingly selective in swinging at pitches. A new rule gave the umpire the authority to call a strike on a batter who continually refused to swing at good pitches. "The umpire," stated the directive, "after warning [the batter], shall call one strike, and if he persists in such action, two and three strikes. When three strikes are called, he shall be subject to the same rules as if he had struck at the three balls."[10]

Since batters now had to swing at pitches in the hitting zone, the advantage went to the pitchers. There was nothing to prevent them from throwing harder, without having to worry about their accuracy, because there was no penalty for throwing "bad" pitches. This changed in 1863. That year, the National Association adopted a rule allowing the umpire to warn a pitcher about making repeated, unhittable throws. If he failed to stop, the umpire could call a "ball." Three of these called balls would award the batter first base.

Over the next quarter century, the rules concerning balls and strikes—and the number which determined a walk or strikeout—were amended several times. In 1870, it was decreed that the umpire no longer had to issue a warning before calling a pitch.

THE BALL

Many fans consider the simple base-ball a sight to behold. "Any baseball is beautiful," wrote author Roger Angell in *Five Seasons.* "No other small package comes as close to the ideal in design and utility. It is a perfect object for a man's hand. Pick it up and it instantly suggests its purpose; it is meant to be thrown a considerable distance—thrown hard and with precision."

More than six hundred thousand base-balls are used by major-league teams during the course of a normal season. Perhaps surprisingly, the average ball remains in play for only five to seven pitches. Home runs, foul balls, and balls that are removed from play after being scuffed account for this relatively short life span.

The major league baseball currently in use has seen remarkably few changes over the past century. It is composed of three basic layers. At the core is a round, cushioned cork center, known as a "pill." It is made of a cork and rubber composition material and is encased in two layers of molded rubber. A thin layer of adhesive is then applied to it.

The pill is then tightly wrapped in three windings of wool and one of polyester/cotton yarn. Wool is the primary material used because of its resiliency. When hit by a bat, the ball quickly becomes compressed, then, just as quickly, returns to its original shape. The polyester/cotton blend gives the sphere added strength.

The final layer consists of two pieces of cowhide cut into figure-eight patterns. Another coating of adhesive is applied to the inside of the cowhide pieces, which are then stitched together with eighty-eight inches of waxed red thread. There are exactly 108 hand-sewn stitches in each ball. The finished product must weigh between five and five and one-fourth ounces and measure between nine and nine and one-fourth inches in circumference.

Despite recent claims from players and managers, there has not been any proof that balls have been "juiced up" in recent years to increase scoring. The only significant change in recent times occurred in 1974, when a shortage in the supply of horses forced a switch from horsehide to cowhide for the covers.

Balls and strikes, however, could not be called on the first toss to a batter. Four years later, a new rule differentiated between a "ball" and a "wide ball." Since 1871, batters had been allowed to call for either a high or low toss from the pitcher, a high one being a ball delivered between the batter's waist and shoulder, and a low one between the knee and waist. In 1874, a "ball" was a pitch not at the height called for by the batter. A "wide ball" was a pitch out of the batter's reach. After three "wides" were called, the batter was awarded first base. On the other hand, only every third ball was called by the umpire. When three such balls (or nine pitches) were thrown, that also constituted a walk. The confusion this caused was eased somewhat the following year. It was then ruled that every third consecutive pitch not over the plate, or at the called-for height, was a ball. Three balls, or nine such pitches, gave the batter first base.

In 1879, the rule was changed so that every ball had to be called, rather than every third one, but nine balls were still required for a walk. This number was amended to eight in 1880, to seven in 1881, to six in 1884, back to seven in 1886, to five in 1887 (a year in which bases on balls were also counted as base hits), and, finally, to the current four in 1889.

A one-year experiment set the number of pitches required for a strikeout to four in 1887. The following year, the number was cut back to three, where it has remained to the present day.

The Strike Zone

The rule defining the limits of the strike zone came under much discussion and saw many changes over the years. In 1867, unfair balls

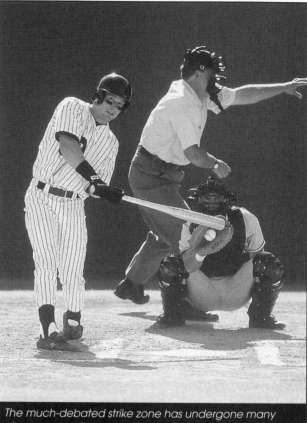

The much-debated strike zone has undergone many changes over the years. Here, a batter is called out on strikes by the home plate umpire.

were defined as, "All pitches striking the ground in front of home base, over the head of the batter, or to the side opposite to that which the batter swings from."[11] With batters able to call for "high" or "low" pitches in 1871, pitches within the called-for height range and over home plate were considered strikes.

In 1887, the rule allowing batters to call for pitches was changed. A strike, or "fair" pitch, was now one which passed over the plate no higher than the batter's shoulder and no lower than his knee. This definition remained basically the same until 1950. That year, the strike zone was shifted to the region between the batter's armpits and the top of his knees when he takes his normal batting stance at the plate. The year 1963 saw the zone return to the area between the top of the batter's shoulders and his knees, then back to between his armpits and the top of his knees six years later.

The question of what is called—or is not called—a strike has been one of the major criticisms of umpires over the years. Players and managers alike complain that the perception of the strike zone varies from umpire to umpire. One man may have a wide zone, while another might "squeeze" the plate, always calling balls on close pitches. Nowadays, however, no matter how the rule reads or who the umpire may be, it is rare for a pitch more than an inch or two above the waist to be called a strike.

Pitching Variations

The style of pitching has also changed significantly. In Cartwright's time, the thrower delivered the ball underhand, with a straight elbow and wrist, from a line forty-five feet from the striker. This line became a "pitcher's box" in 1863. Four years later, the pitcher's delivery was spelled out more exactly as a pitch, rather than a jerked or thrown ball. "A pitched ball is one delivered with arm straight and swinging . . . [parallel] and free from the body,"[12] read the rule. A jerked ball was one thrown with a snap of the wrist, while a thrown ball was any one executed with an overhand motion.

The curveball was legalized in 1872. The jerk, wrist snap, and bent-elbow deliveries

---

CANDY CUMMINGS AND THE CURVEBALL

The ongoing battle between pitcher and hitter was affected by the development of the curveball as much as by any rule change. Cap Anson, arguably the greatest hitter of the nineteenth century, called the pitch "the greatest change ever made in the National Game." Like the origin of baseball itself, the origin of this "trick" pitch has been shrouded by the mists of time. Although several pitchers laid claims to it, William Arthur "Candy" Cummings is usually credited with its discovery.

Born in Ware, Massachusetts, in 1848, Cummings and his family moved to the baseball hotbed of Brooklyn, New York, when he was just a youngster. He reportedly developed the baffling pitch after watching the flight of clamshells that he tossed into the wind on a nearby beach. After hours of experimentation on his neighborhood friends, he eventually achieved the hoped-for result by applying various degrees of pressure on the ball with his middle finger.

In 1867, while hurling for the Brooklyn Excelsior Juniors, Cummings successfully used the pitch in a game for the first time. As the opposing Harvard club flailed futilely at his pitches, he could hardly contain his elation. He described his feelings in an interview years later: "I curve balled them to death. I wanted to tell everybody. It was too good to keep to myself. But I said not a word, and I saw many a batter at that game throw down his stick in disgust. Every time I was successful, I could scarcely keep from dancing for joy."

Cummings went on to establish himself as one of the top amateur players of the day. He entered the professional ranks and enjoyed his best year with Hartford of the National Association in 1875 (35–12, 1.60 ERA). For his contributions to the game, he was elected to the Baseball Hall of Fame in 1939.

---

were approved, as long as the pitcher kept his hand lower than his hip while moving forward. Overhand and "round arm" throws were still forbidden. In 1883, a pitch was declared legal as long as it did not pass above the line of the pitcher's shoulder. By the following year, all restrictions on the pitcher's delivery had been lifted, and overhand throws were allowed for the first time.

The pitcher's rubber made its debut in 1893. The rubber is a rectangular slab of white rubber, set crosswise on the pitcher's mound. The pitcher must remain in contact with it while throwing a pitch. At the same time, the distance from the rubber to home plate was moved back to its current sixty feet, six inches. A decade later, the elevation of the pitcher's box was set at no more than fifteen inches higher than the baselines and home plate. In 1969, following a season in which pitchers dominated hitters, the height of the pitcher's rubber on the mound was lowered to ten inches above the level of home plate. It remains at that level today, although teams occasionally try to heighten it in order to give their pitchers an advantage.

Defaced Balls

A further matter which had a direct effect on the pitcher-batter confrontation was the issue of defaced baseballs. Pitchers have always looked to obtain any advantage possible over hitters. This might be as innocent as rubbing dirt on a ball to make it harder to see, or as flagrantly illegal as cutting the sphere with a ring.

Umpires have always been allowed to remove a ball from play if it was ripped or drastically out of shape. In many cases, however, a single ball lasted an entire game, becoming more and more defaced by dirt, mud, and scratches as the contest progressed. It was not until 1890 that a rule was adopted making it illegal to intentionally discolor the ball. As more imaginative hurlers experimented with applying a wider variety of substances to the ball's surface, it became necessary to take further action.

In 1920, a rule was instituted which made it illegal to discolor the ball "by rubbing it with the soil, or by applying rosin, paraffin, licorice, or any other foreign substance to it, or otherwise intentionally damaging or roughening the same with sandpaper or emery paper, or other substance."[13] For violating this pronouncement, the pitcher was to be removed from the game and suspended for a period of ten days. Over the years, several pitchers had become extremely proficient at applying moisture to a ball in order to make it dip and drop. For these hurlers, the rule would have been a death sentence. Major-league baseball agreed to allow those "certified" spitball pitchers who were active at the time to be exempt from the rule, as it related to the spitball, for the duration of their careers.

Since then, numerous hurlers have admitted to "loading one up" every now and then,

Hall of Famer Gaylord Perry being the most famous. "Gaylord is a very honorable man," former Cleveland Indians president Gabe Paul once explained. "He only calls for the spitball when he needs it."[14] Only rarely, however, have any been caught in the act and punished by the "men in blue." Modern times have seen pitchers become more ingenious in finding ways to deface the ball and escape detection. Scratching it with a thumbtack taped to a finger, a piece of sandpaper hidden in a glove, or a sharpened belt buckle are three of the more inventive methods used.

Other Significant Rule Changes

Aside from those rule changes affecting the pitcher and batter, there have been relatively few major adjustments to the game of baseball since the 1860s. Rules have been clarified, refined, and expanded upon over the years, and a 1950 revision saw the entire code essentially rewritten. Still, a modern-day fan would have no trouble at all following the action in a late-nineteenth-century contest.

One of those major changes had been experimented with for many years until it finally became official in 1865. That was the rule which mandated that a batted ball be caught by a fielder on the fly—and not on one bounce—to be declared an out. This was, of course, more challenging, and necessitated superior skills. By 1895, the use of gloves had become widespread, as an aid to fielding more than as protection for a player's hands. It became common practice for fielders to leave their gloves on the field between innings when their team was at bat. It was not until 1954 that this custom was abolished.

The most significant change of modern times occurred in 1973. On April 6th of that

Hall of Famer Gaylord Perry, one of the numerous pitchers who has admitted to occasionally doctoring a baseball.

year, Ron Blomberg of the New York Yankees became baseball's first official designated hitter (DH). The DH came into being in an effort to spark an increase in scoring. The ruling allowed a team to designate a hitter to bat for the starting pitcher in a game—and all subsequent pitchers—without having to play in the field. This rule was adopted by the American League, as well as all minor leagues, but not by the

THE MERKLE BONER

Although a rule may be part of baseball's official code, that does not mean it is always enforced. Usually—as in the case of the statute which says a pitcher must deliver a pitch within twenty seconds—the rule has little, if any, effect on the outcome of a game. In one instance, however, the enforcement of such a rule affected the outcome of a pennant race.

In 1908, the Chicago Cubs and New York Giants were in contention for the National League pennant. A September game between the Cubs and the Pittsburgh Pirates found the teams tied, 0–0, in the bottom of the tenth inning. When the home team Pirates scored what appeared to be the winning run, the runner on first base ran off the field, as was the custom of the day, rather than proceed to second base. Chicago second baseman Johnny Evers retrieved the ball and stepped on the bag, complaining to umpire Hank O'Day that the runner should be out on a force play since he never reached the next base safely. According to the rule book, this would have nullified the winning run. Unfortunately for the Cubs, O'Day said he did not see the play and allowed the run to stand.

Later that month, the Cubs and Giants were locked in a tense battle. The game was tied at one run apiece as the Giants batted in the last half of the ninth inning. Fred Merkle, New York's nineteen-year-old first baseman, was on first when Al Bridwell singled home what appeared to be the winning run. As the fans streamed onto the field, Merkle watched the winning run score, then ran toward the clubhouse with the rest of his teammates. Second baseman Evers once again noticed the failure of the runner to touch second. As luck would have it, Hank O'Day was again one of the umpires. Evers eventually retrieved the ball and stepped on the base. O'Day, being prepared for the situation, called Merkle out. The run did not count, and the game remained tied.

By now, however, the fans had mobbed the field and continuation of play was impossible. Despite protests by the Giants, National League president Harry Pulliam ruled the contest a tie. It was decided that the game would be replayed only if its outcome affected the pennant race.

As luck would have it, the Cubs and Giants finished the season tied for first with identical 98–55 records. The makeup game had to be played to decide the pennant. The Cubs went on to defeat New York, 4–2, behind the pitching of Mordecai "Three-Finger" Brown. They advanced to the World Series, where they played—and defeated—Ty Cobb and the Detroit Tigers for the world championship. The play which decided that September game became known forever after as "Merkle's Boner." Perhaps it should better be remembered as "Evers's Epiphany."

Ron Blomberg, baseball's first official designated hitter.

National League. Since that time, the two major leagues have, in effect, been playing different games. Although scoring has indeed increased in the American League, the rule is denounced by many who claim it nullifies the need for many strategic decisions. The need for a single rule for both leagues becomes obvious in the World Series. Baseball's ultimate encounter is played under two sets of rules, depending on which of the clubs involved is the home team. Such an outrageous situation exists in no other major team sport.

CHAPTER 3

Improving the Game's Image

IN JUNE OF 1875, forty-two-year-old coal merchant William Ambrose Hulbert was elected president of the Chicago White Stockings of the National Association. Within the year, he became the driving force behind the organization of the National League of Professional Base Ball Clubs, the successor to the corrupt, unstable National Association. The organization signified a shift in power from the athletes themselves to the businessmen who owned the teams. This new system would prevail for the next century.

The National League

Hulbert knew that to make his new league a success—and, at the same time, a profitable enterprise—he had to improve the game's image. Gambling, cheating, and rowdiness could not be tolerated, nor could the instability of member clubs or the practice of players jumping teams. Toward these ends, the league instituted a number of reforms. Teams were allowed to "reserve" five of their players. Other clubs agreed not to negotiate with these players, meaning the owners would not try to sign players who were under contract to another team. This prevented a player from jumping from one club to another and helped to maintain salary levels. This was the beginning of the reserve system which helped establish management's control over the players for the better part of a century.

In order to encourage team stability, membership in the league was limited to eight franchises. These were the strongest clubs from the cities of Boston, Chicago,

Cincinnati, Hartford, Louisville, New York, Philadelphia, and St. Louis. Smaller cities were kept out through strict membership requirements. Clubs were awarded exclusive rights in their areas, becoming limited monopolies.

To attract more fans—and a better class of fan—the league banned gambling and liquor sales in its parks, as well as playing games on Sundays. It promised to end rowdy behavior, and did so, in part by strengthening the role of the umpire.

Hulbert's measures to improve the integrity of the game were successful, but not so his efforts at curbing team instability. Income was down and unemployment was widespread. There was a general imbalance of strength between the stronger and weaker teams, as well as competition from minor leagues and independent teams. As a result, attendance slumped and teams were forced to fold. In its first fifteen years of existence, the National League fielded teams in twenty-two different cities.

THE LOUISVILLE GRAYS SCANDAL OF 1877

With the Louisville Grays atop the National League standings by five and a half games in late-August of 1877, it appeared the team was on its way to the league championship. Suddenly, however, the club could do no right. During an eastern road trip, sloppy play was the rule of the day. The Grays quickly lost eight games in a row and fell to second place behind the Boston squad.

The Louisville newspapers became suspicious, and rumors of a fix began to surface. Louisville vice president Charles Chase received warnings that gamblers were betting heavily against the Grays. He began questioning several players whose names had been mentioned. The first—star pitcher Jim Devlin—admitted to throwing an exhibition game, but denied anything further. Slugging outfielder George Hall, believing Devlin had already confessed, acknowledged fixing several contests. Hall also pointed the finger at utility infielder Al Nichols as the ringleader. Chase requested permission from the players to inspect all

telegrams they had received. Infielder Bill Craver refused, but the others agreed under the threat of expulsion from the team.

An examination of the telegrams, which contained coded words and messages, confirmed the plot. Devlin, Hall, and Nichols were expelled for their parts in the conspiracy. Craver, who had been accused of throwing games earlier in his career, was banished for his refusal to cooperate in the investigation. Later that year, the league upheld the expulsions at its winter meeting. The four players were banned from baseball for life. Devlin, for one, repeatedly begged National League president William Hulbert for reinstatement, but all for naught. "Damn you, Devlin," exclaimed Hulbert on one occasion, as reported in *Baseball,* by Geoffrey C. Ward and Ken Burns, "you are dishonest; you have sold a game, and I can't trust you. Now go; and let me never see your face again; for your act will not be condoned so long as I live." By his actions, Hulbert gave notice to all that he was serious about cleaning up baseball's poor image.

Boston and Chicago were the only franchises to remain afloat throughout that entire period.

The American Association

By 1880, the economy had been revived, and so, too, had the fortunes of the National League. With many teams unable to gain entrance to the circuit, the time was ripe for a new major league to enter the fray. Thus, in 1882, the American Association began play, fielding teams in Cincinnati, Louisville, St. Louis, Baltimore, Pittsburgh, and Philadelphia. The new league tried to appeal to the working man, allowing beer, for example, to be served at its games.

After a period in which the American Association actively went after players in the more established league, a truce was arrived at in 1884. As part of the settlement, a postseason exhibition series between the champions of the two leagues was agreed upon. This was a precursor to the World Series of today.

At first, the American Association fared well in its rivalry with the established league. By 1890, however, its prospects had dimmed considerably. Despite the cooperation between the leagues, there was still keen competition for star players. As a result, salaries increased significantly. With a low admission price of twenty-five cents (as opposed to fifty cents in the National League), American Association franchises found it hard to compete successfully with the older organization. The league was forced to shut down operations following the 1891 season. Four of its more successful clubs were absorbed into the National League, increasing the older circuit's membership to twelve.

The American Association was not the only competition that faced the National League. By 1883, the reserve rule had been expanded to cover as many as eleven players per team, up from the original five. As owners gained more and more control, players grew more and more resentful. The Union Association gave the players another choice. "We do not believe in the 11-man reserve rule," wrote league secretary William W. White. "That is our cornerstone."[15] Lack of fan interest, however, caused the league to fold after just one season (1884).

With competition between the National League and American Association causing the salary structure to shift upward, the owners took it upon themselves in 1886 to set a two-thousand-dollar ceiling on the pay scale. The enraged players once again looked elsewhere for help in their struggles with ownership.

The Players' League

The National Brotherhood of Professional Baseball Players was conceived in 1885 as an organization dedicated to caring for needy players. It soon became involved in championing the rights of its ninety members, taking on the character of a labor union. New York Giants shortstop John Montgomery Ward led the Brotherhood's fight against what it considered to be the inequities of the reserve system, as well as other issues. "There is now no escape for the player," wrote Ward. "If he attempts to elude the operation of the rule, he becomes at once a professional outlaw, and the hand of every club is against him."[16] At first, the owners seemed amenable to changes requested by the players. In time, however, negotiations between the two sides deteriorated. Following the 1889 season, the players decided to form a league of their own. The Players' League was established in November and began play the next year.

The Players' League was able to attract many of the leading players of the day and its outlook for success seemed bright. The more powerful National League fought back aggressively. Ticket prices were slashed, and attendance rose in both circuits. The Players' League, however, could not afford to continue its battle with the wealthier National League. A settlement was negotiated, but all to the benefit of the older league. The reserve system remained in place, and a salary cap was

established. By the end of 1891, the National League once again had a monopoly.

The Baltimore Orioles and "Scientific" Baseball

The decade of the 1890s saw dramatic changes take place on the field of play. The pitching distance was increased to its current dimensions, with a resulting surge in hitting. "Scientific," or "inside," baseball became popular, best exemplified by the play of the Baltimore Orioles. Baltimore,

Baseball stars such as Wee Willie Keeler (pictured) attempted to outsmart opponents by utilizing the bunt, squeeze play, stolen base, and hit and run.

led by stars such as John McGraw, Wilbert Robinson, and Wee Willie Keeler, employed the bunt, squeeze play, hit-and-run, and stolen base to previously unheard-of degrees. Rather than overpowering their opponents, they tried to outsmart them. The club did so by employing a roughhouse, aggressive style of play which intimidated and dominated the opposition. Knocking down batters with pitches, sliding into bases with spikes flying high, and deliberately tripping base runners were just some of the strategies used by teams looking to gain an edge over their opponents. Fans enjoyed this new approach. "Sportsmanship and easygoing methods are all right," theorized McGraw, "but it is the prospect of a hot fight that brings out the crowds."[17]

The rowdiness which characterized this era's style of play was due to a combination of factors. In part, it may have been a result of player frustration and feelings of helplessness from recent dealings with management. It also reflected the changing ethnic makeup of the league. With many more European immigrants—especially Irish and German—playing ball, ethnic and religious confrontations occasionally spilled out into the open. Irish Catholics, in particular, became a common target of opposing Protestant players.

The fans were also quick to get into the act. Drinking and gambling had gradually made their way back into the game. Fans who had more to lose when a call went against their team did not hesitate to heap abuse on the umpires. Physical confrontations on the field were not at all uncommon.

The 1890s also saw the onset of what was known as syndicatism, in which several owners had controlling interests in more than one team. This allowed them to move players from one club to another in an effort to strengthen a favored team. This resulted in a few clubs rising to the top of the standings and others dropping hopelessly out of contention.

With attendance down throughout the league, it became obvious that changes were in order. The league's answer was to drop four of its teams, reducing the number of clubs to a more manageable eight. This grouping—consisting of the Boston Beaneaters, Brooklyn Superbas, Chicago Cubs, Cincinnati Reds, New York Giants, Philadelphia Phillies, Pittsburgh Pirates, and St. Louis Cardinals—would remain intact for more than half a century. A bigger challenge to the National League's monopoly, however, was already taking shape.

Ban Johnson and the American League

In 1894, former sportswriter Byron Bancroft "Ban" Johnson was named president of the Western League, a minor circuit based in the Midwest. Johnson's dream was to raise his association to major-league status. He built it up financially, then, in late 1899, changed its name to the American League.

THE 1899 CLEVELAND SPIDERS

In a glaring example of syndicate baseball, the Robison brothers, owners of the Cleveland Spiders, gained control of the St. Louis Browns franchise just prior to the start of the 1899 season. They renamed the team the Perfectos and relocated several Cleveland players west to St. Louis. The move ultimately proved fatal to the Spiders.

Cleveland went on to compile the all-time worst single-season record in baseball history, winning just 20 games while losing 134. The team, which had finished in fifth place in the twelve-team National League in 1898, dropped into last place, 84 games behind the league-leading Brooklyn squad. St. Louis, on the other hand, performed the exact opposite maneuver, jumping from the basement up into fifth place.

The Spiders did their best on the field, but the talent simply was not there. They finished at the bottom of the league in virtually every offensive category, scoring at least two hundred fewer runs than every other team. The pitching was not any better. The staff was led by Jim Hughey (4–30), rookie Charlie Knepper (4–22), Frederick "Crazy" Schmit (2–17), Frank Bates (1–18), and Harry Colliflower (1–11). The Spiders compiled six losing streaks of 11 or more games, with a National League record 24 as their high.

Cleveland fans, disgusted by their club's ineptitude, stayed away from the ballpark in droves. So poor was the attendance that most of the games in the second half of the season had to be played on the road. Nothing seemed to help, however. The Spiders finished the month of September with a record of 1–27.

The National League cut back to eight teams in 1900, with Cleveland being one of the casualties. The Spiders' atrocious final season can be put in better perspective when compared with that of the most famous modern losers, the expansion New York Mets of 1962. If the Spiders had finished with the same record that season, they would have come in seventeen games behind the woeful New Yorkers.

When the National League announced its plan to drop four teams for the 1900 season, Johnson made his move. He placed a new franchise in Chicago, under the ownership of Charles Comiskey, to compete with the Cubs. Four new teams—the Baltimore Orioles, Boston Somersets, Philadelphia Athletics, and Washington Nationals—were established in eastern cities, joining the Chicago White Stockings, Cleveland Blues, Detroit Tigers, and Milwaukee Brewers in the eight-team circuit.

Johnson had teams sign former players who had been cut loose by the National League clubs, and encouraged them to raid National League rosters of current stars. To the players, he promised higher salaries; to the fans, he promised a more wholesome atmosphere in which to watch the players perform.

Despite protests and lawsuits by National League owners, the American League flourished. Following a triumphant 1900 season, Johnson took it upon himself to proclaim the

The American League flourished under the leadership of Byron Bancroft "Ban" Johnson.

American League a major league. "The American League," boasted Johnson, "will be the principal organization of the country within a very short time. Mark my prediction!"[18] Dozens more National League players jumped to the new circuit in 1901, including stars such as Nap Lajoie, Cy Young, and Jimmy Collins.

The following year, with the American League threatening to place a franchise in New York City, the National League sued for peace. The National Agreement of 1903 was negotiated, ending the three-year war between the leagues. The agreement stipulated that the two circuits would conduct

their business as separate but equal major leagues. A common set of rules would be adhered to by the two leagues, and an understanding was reached that raids on players would end. Johnson was allowed to move the Baltimore franchise to New York, where it was renamed the Highlanders (and eventually became the Yankees). The Milwaukee franchise also relocated, becoming the St. Louis Browns. The resulting eight-team configuration would remain in place for the next fifty years.

National League and American League negotiators also agreed to create a three-man National Committee to enforce the rules laid out by the agreement. League presidents Ban Johnson and Henry Pulliam were joined on the Committee by a permanent chairman, Garry Herrmann, a longtime friend of Johnson's. As a result, Johnson emerged as the most powerful figure on the major-league scene.

The World Series

With two equal leagues now on the scene, it seemed only natural that some sort of postseason competition would be devised to determine an overall champion. In 1903, the two league winners—Boston and Pittsburgh—agreed to play a nine-game series, which was won by the Pilgrims (as the Somersets were also known). Some die-hard National Leaguers, however, rejected the American League's claim to equal standing. The 1904 New York Giants thus refused to face Boston following the 1904 season. The resulting public outcry caused the leagues to adopt a best-of-seven World Series format to begin after the 1905 season. Under the control of the National Committee, the plan proved successful. The World Series became a permanent, important conclusion to the major league campaign.

For the better part of the first two decades of the new century, peace and prosperity reigned throughout baseball. The game's popularity and attendance benefited by increased media coverage. The 1908 Jack Norworth song, "Take Me Out to the Ball Game," also served to embed the sport in the nation's consciousness. Scientific baseball continued to have a strong influence, personified by the top stars of the day, including Ty Cobb, Tris Speaker, Honus Wagner, and Nap Lajoie. For the most part, however, pitching dominated. Cy Young, Walter Johnson, and Christy Mathewson stood at the top of the game's elite corps of moundsmen.

Baseball's coming of age was symbolized by the construction of several new concrete ballparks. Fifteen of these new edifices were raised between the years of 1909 and 1923, becoming civic monuments in their communities. More

fans could watch games in comfort and safety, producing even more revenue for the owners. This, in turn, allowed them to pay higher salaries to star players.

Baseball's solidarity enabled it to fight off a brief challenge from the upstart Federal League. This new "major" league lasted but two seasons—1914 and 1915—before financial losses took their toll on ownership. No new league has mounted a successful challenge to the two established leagues since that time.

Legendary pitcher Cy Young dominated hitters in the early-twentieth century.

A new hurdle for baseball to overcome, however, came in the form of World War I. Dozens of players left to serve in the military, and the leagues played shortened schedules in both 1918 and 1919. When the war ended, team owners tried to recover some of the money they had lost by expanding the World Series to a best-of-nine-game format for 1919. The Series that year, however, provided a far more serious crisis to be faced.

The Black Sox Scandal

Even before the Series began, rumors surfaced about the possibility of a fix being on. "Advise all not to bet on this Series," wired sportswriter Hugh Fullerton to papers carrying his column. "Ugly rumors afloat." [19] The Chicago White Sox were the overwhelming favorites to defeat the National League champion Cincinnati Reds. The week prior to the Series, however, large amounts of money were bet on the underdog Reds. When Chicago lost the Series, five games to three, suspicions became stronger. In order to refute the rumors, Chicago owner Charles Comiskey offered a substantial reward for proof that any players were involved in throwing games. No evidence was forthcoming, and the rumors died down.

Nearly a year later, on September 4, 1920, questions arose concerning a possible fix in a Phillies-Cubs game. An Illinois grand jury convened to investigate gambling in baseball. Philadelphia gambler Billy Maharg was one of those called in for questioning. Upset because he had not received his promised cut in the Series fix, Maharg revealed the plot and implicated eight Chicago players. According to him, the players were to receive a total of one hundred thousand dollars, most of which was never delivered. The players had agreed to the fix because of the stinginess of owner Comiskey. With salaries having been cut due to the war, the money promised the players was more than their earnings.

The following day, two of the accused players—pitcher Ed Cicotte and outfielder Joe Jackson—broke down before the grand jury and confessed to the scheme. "I done it for the wife and kiddies," [20] explained Cicotte. A trial for the eight players implicated—Cicotte, Jackson, third baseman Buck Weaver, shortstop Swede Risberg, first baseman Chick Gandil (considered to be the ringleader), outfielder Happy Felsch, pitcher Claude "Lefty" Williams, and utility man Fred McMullin—was set for July of the following year.

By the time the trial rolled around, however, the confessions had mysteriously disappeared. The players denied any roles in the fix, and after several hours of deliberation, the jury acquitted each of them of all charges. Newly appointed baseball czar Kenesaw Mountain Landis, however, was not convinced.

Landis had been a federal district judge, with a reputation for being strict. In recent

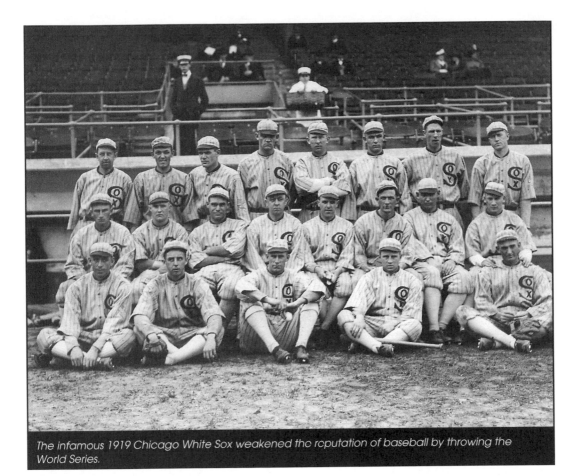

The infamous 1919 Chicago White Sox weakened the reputation of baseball by throwing the World Series.

years, fights among the owners had weakened the authority of the three-man National Committee. When rumors of the Series scandal threatened to destroy the game, the owners turned to Landis to restore public confidence. They gave him powers virtually without limit, including "to investigate, either upon complaint or upon his own initiative, any act, transaction, or practice . . . suspected to be detrimental to the best interests of the national game of baseball."[21] Landis officially took over as baseball's commissioner on January 21, 1921.

During the course of the 1921 season, Landis handed down several decisions which served to validate his authority. He showed no mercy in meting out the severest penalties to those whom he thought posed any threat to the national pastime. In March, he barred former major-league pitcher Gene Paulette for taking part in throwing games. Less than two months later, Giants outfielder—and former Federal League batting champion—Benny Kauff became a victim. Kauff had been arrested on charges of auto theft but was acquitted. Landis, however, banned him for life because of his "undesirable" character and reputation. Finally, in mid-June, pitcher Ray Fisher was permanently placed on the ineligible list for alleged contract jumping.

When the Black Sox trial ended in early August, Landis made his most important decision. The eight players involved were barred from organized baseball for life, despite their acquittal by the jury. Landis was emphatic in his ruling. "Regardless of the verdict of juries," he declared, "no player that throws a ball game; no player that sits in a conference with a bunch of crooked players and gamblers where the ways and means of throwing games are discussed, and does not promptly tell his club about it, will ever play professional ball."[22] His reputation as baseball's great protector was set firmly in place.

Babe Ruth and the Lively Ball

Although some consider Judge Landis to have been baseball's savior, many more believe Babe Ruth is best deserving of that title. The Bambino, as Ruth was known, helped launch baseball into its golden age and became the most dominating figure in the game's history.

Ruth came up to the major leagues in 1914 as a left-handed pitcher with the Boston Red Sox. He quickly became one of the game's outstanding hurlers, twice winning more than twenty games in a season, and helping Boston to world championships in 1915, 1916, and 1918. Ruth's ability to hit a baseball, however, was even greater than his ability to throw one.

In 1918, while playing the outfield and first base when he was not on the mound, Ruth clouted 11 home runs to tie for the major league lead. The following year, he slugged an even more impressive 29 round-trippers for a new record.

At the end of the year, financially-strapped Boston owner Harry Frazee sold Ruth to the New York Yankees in exchange for $125,000 in cash and a $300,000 loan. That sale was perhaps the all-time greatest blunder in the history of sports. Ruth proceeded to rewrite the record books and lead the New Yorkers to one world title after another. The Yankee juggernaut powered its way to victory after victory, with the home run as its most intimidating weapon. Fans came out in droves to watch the "Sultan of Swat" blast balls into the seats.

In 1920, the Babe nearly doubled his previous record by swatting an incredible 54 home runs. Only one other *team,* aside from the Yankees, hit that many for the season. The following year he topped his mark again, slugging 59 round-trippers and driving home 171 runs while batting a robust .378. Six years later, he surpassed his own record one final time. He belted 60 home runs that year, a number that would take on

Babe Ruth's home run proficiency brought fans out to the ballpark in record numbers.

an almost mystical aura over the succeeding decades. That 1927 Yankees team is considered by most historians to be the greatest team of all time.

Ruth brought fans out to the ballpark in record numbers. The salary he earned from playing ball and from outside endorsements dwarfed the earnings of other stars of the day. His effect on the game of baseball cannot be minimized.

Branch Rickey and the Farm System

Powered by Ruth, Lou Gehrig, Tony Lazzeri, and Bob Meusel, the Yankees of the 1920s won six pennants and three world championships. They established themselves as the team against which all future dynasties would be measured. With fans pouring through the turnstiles in record numbers, the Yankees quickly became the wealthiest major league franchise. This allowed them to purchase players from other minor and major league clubs in order to replenish their team with high-quality performers. In this way, they were able to continue producing pennant-contending teams on a regular basis. In the 1930s, this translated into five more pennants and world titles, including four in a row from 1936 through 1939.

Meanwhile, over in the National League, a new dynasty was emerging in St. Louis. The Cardinals won their first championship in 1926, then proceeded to win four more pennants and two more world titles over the next ten years. St. Louis, however, was conducting its business differently. Cardinals general manager Branch Rickey realized his team could not compete with the larger market clubs, like the Yankees and Giants of New York. Instead of buying players when he needed them, he decided to cultivate them himself. "Starting the Cardinal farm system was no sudden stroke of genius," explained Rickey. "It was a case of necessity being the mother of invention. We lived a precarious existence. Other clubs would outbid us; they had the money and the superior scouting system. We had to take the leavings or nothing at all."[23]

Prior to Rickey, most minor-league teams were independently owned. These teams scouted, signed, and developed their own players. If a player reached star status, a major-league team might make an offer to buy him. An owner, however, might occasionally refuse to sell his stars, preferring

NIGHT BASEBALL

Many fans know that the first night baseball game in major-league history took place in Cincinnati in 1935. What many do not know is that the first experimental games played under the lights were held more than half a century earlier.

On September 2, 1880—less than a year after Edison invented the incandescent bulb—teams representing two Boston department stores played a game at Nantasket Beach, Massachusetts. The game was staged by the Northern Electric Light Company in an attempt to demonstrate how electricity could be used in outdoor settings. The twelve lamps that were used produced a total of just thirty thousand candlepower. The results encouraged further experiments in the ensuing years.

In 1909, George, Thaddeus, and Arthur Cahill devised a portable lighting system. Exhibition games played under the system that year and the next were considered successes, but major-league owners still refused to take the idea of night baseball seriously.

The year 1927 saw another experiment win raves. A game between two Class B teams was played at West Lynn, Massachusetts, under a lighting system installed by General Electric. Representatives of the major leagues who were in attendance came back with favorable reviews of the contest. Washington Senators All-Star outfielder Goose Goslin went so far as to state his desire to play in such a game in the future. Within three years, three leagues were vying for the honor of hosting the first regular-season game to be played under lights.

The historic event finally occurred on Monday, April 28, 1930. About 1,000 fans came out to see Muskogee defeat Independence by a score of 13–3 in a Class C Western Association contest. Other clubs began to install lights as teams began to realize that night baseball increased attendance.

The major leagues finally joined the bandwagon in 1935. Cincinnati's Crosley Field became the first major-league park to be equipped with lights. On May 24, 1935, 20,422 people were in attendance as President Franklin D. Roosevelt pushed a button from the White House which flooded the field with light. National League president Ford Frick threw out the first ball, and the Reds proceeded to defeat the Philadelphia Phillies, 2–1. Baseball had entered a new era.

instead to establish a minor-league dynasty of his own.

Major-league baseball, like other businesses, was hard hit by the Great Depression. Player salaries were cut as attendance at ballparks dropped significantly. For Rickey, this was the perfect opportunity. He signed as many young prospects as he could, for salaries as low as three hundred dollars per season. By 1936, the Cardinals owned twenty-eight minor-league teams at different levels; in 1929, they had owned but five. In so doing, Rickey developed a farm system of teams that kept supplying his major-league club with young stars. Surplus players were often sold to other major league teams, bringing in additional income to St. Louis.

With the Cardinals' farm system producing spectacular results, other teams began to follow suit. The 1930s became known as the golden age of minor-league baseball. As the farm system network grew, however, so, too, did Judge Landis's opposition to it.

Landis believed that the idea of a farm system hurt baseball. Fans in every small town and village across the nation took pride in supporting a team they could call their own. It was not unusual for a major-league club to call up a player when his team was in the middle of a pennant race. It was detrimental to the game, argued Landis, for the loyal fans of such a minor-league club to suddenly find themselves without a star they had supported for most of the season.

In the 1930s, Cardinals general manager Branch Rickey cultivated the farm system in order to compete with larger market teams.

Additionally, a team could "hide" a player in its system, thereby hindering his chances of making it to the major leagues. The belief that this was a violation of a player's rights caused Landis to grant free agency to seventy-four St. Louis minor leaguers in 1938, and to dozens of Detroit Tigers prospects two years later. By the time World War II began, the wide-ranging Rickey-style farm system had passed its zenith and begun its decline.

Branch Rickey's impact on major-league baseball was not over, however. Within a few short years, he would be instrumental in bringing about a change that would alter the face of the game forever.

CHAPTER 4

Burning Issues

The modern game of baseball has seen players shake off their shackles through free agency and put an end to decades of exploitation at the hands of owners. Before that could be done, however, other forms of discrimination had to be challenged.

The Negro Leagues

Although professional baseball had opened its doors to players of nearly every nationality, one group unable to take advantage of this opportunity was African Americans. Blacks had performed on several lower-level pro teams as early as the 1870s, with John Fowler credited with being the first black professional player. The National Association and National League, however, had unofficial bans against blacks. The 1880s saw several blacks dot the rosters of minor-league clubs, and two brothers—Moses and Welday Walker—even made appearances for the Toledo club of the major-league American Association in 1884.

This apparent easing of restrictions came to an end in 1887. When several International League teams began fielding black players, some whites began to protest. Tensions reached their height in 1887 when Cap Anson's Chicago White Stockings were scheduled to play an exhibition game against the International League's Newark club. Newark was led by its star black pitcher, George Stovey, called "the greatest African-American pitcher of the nineteenth century"[24] by baseball historian Jerry Malloy. The racist Anson refused to let his team take the field against an integrated squad. Newark dropped Stovey from its roster at the end of the season, and the ban on blacks soon became an unofficial policy.

The major leagues' policy toward blacks mirrored the general feelings among whites in most parts of the country at the time. Few objected to the formation of all-black teams or leagues, but integration was frowned upon. This policy would remain in effect for more than half a century.

Baseball people recognized the athletic talents and abilities of black players even while segregation was the norm. In 1901,

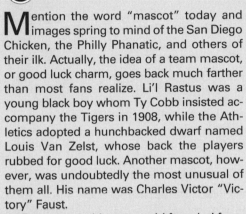

VICTORY FAUST

Mention the word "mascot" today and images spring to mind of the San Diego Chicken, the Philly Phanatic, and others of their ilk. Actually, the idea of a team mascot, or good luck charm, goes back much farther than most fans realize. Li'l Rastus was a young black boy whom Ty Cobb insisted accompany the Tigers in 1908, while the Athletics adopted a hunchbacked dwarf named Louis Van Zelst, whose back the players rubbed for good luck. Another mascot, however, was undoubtedly the most unusual of them all. His name was Charles Victor "Victory" Faust.

Faust was a thirty-year-old farm lad from Kansas. In the Spring of 1911, he was told by a fortune-teller that if he went to the New York Giants baseball team, he would pitch them to the pennant. Considered by many locals to be slightly retarded, or at the least eccentric, Faust set out to fulfill his destiny. He traveled to St. Louis, where on July 28 he approached Giants manager John McGraw and related his story. Surprisingly, McGraw gave him a tryout.

It did not take long for McGraw to see that Faust was not a ballplayer. The manager decided to have a little fun with him and put him through his paces as the players and fans smiled at his ineptitude. In an effort to loosen his team up, McGraw allowed Faust to dress up on the bench. Almost immediately, the team went on a winning streak and surged into first place. With his antics on the field before games keeping the fans amused, the team adopted him as its unofficial mascot. Faust, however, was dead serious about being a ballplayer, and warmed up before each game in the belief he was going to pitch.

Later that year, Faust's newfound fame got him a job in vaudeville. He left the team, and the Giants promptly lost three games. He returned to the club and the Giants regained their winning ways. After New York clinched the pennant, McGraw even allowed Faust to make brief appearances in two games. The Giants proceeded to lose the World Series, however, and his magic seemed to have worn off.

He returned in 1912, but not as a player. With Faust on the bench for much of the season, the Giants once again won the pennant, but lost the World Series. McGraw dismissed him the next season in an effort to make his players believe more in their own abilities and less in their "good luck charm." The Giants managed to win again in 1913, but dropped to second place the next year.

Despite repeated letters to the Giants asking to be brought back, Faust's days as a mascot were over. He disappeared from sight until resurfacing in an insane asylum in late 1914. He died there in June 1915.

That year, the Giants finished in last place.

Baltimore manager John Mc-Graw tried to pass off a black infielder named Charlie Grant as an American Indian. Several years later, the Cincinnati Reds signed two light-skinned Cubans who may well have been of mixed ancestry.

With the major leagues unavailable to them, blacks formed their own teams and barnstormed around the country. The success of these teams led to the formation of several black leagues. An important figure in this movement was Andrew "Rube" Foster. Foster had been a dominating pitcher in his days as a player before moving on to the management side of the game. In 1920, he organized the Negro National League, placing teams in several large cities.

Pitcher Satchel Page and other Negro league players often won more games than they lost against white All-Star teams.

After a slow beginning, black baseball picked up momentum. The Negro American League was formed in 1937 by Gus Greenlee, and the years that followed saw black baseball reach its peak of popularity.

Players in the Negro leagues were undoubtedly equal in ability to their counterparts in the majors. Stars such as Josh Gibson, Buck Leonard, Cool Papa Bell, and Satchel Paige occasionally played in exhibitions against white All-Star teams, often winning more games than they lost.

As the 1940s approached, many blacks began to migrate to northern cities. These potential customers gave major-league owners a new reason to consider breaking the ban. When dozens of big leaguers left for military service in World War II, they found themselves fighting for the same cause as blacks. Many wondered aloud why it was acceptable for blacks to go into battle with whites, but not to compete with them on the playing field. Baseball commissioner Happy Chandler was one who agreed. "If a black boy can make it at Okinawa and go to Guadalcanal," said Chandler, "he can make it in baseball."[25]

Branch Rickey and the "Great Experiment"

Such was the prevailing atmosphere around the major leagues when Branch Rickey took over as president of the Brooklyn Dodgers in the early 1940s. Rickey saw the chance to improve his team while at the same time righting a wrong that had been enacted against a significant portion of society since before the turn of the century. "My only purpose is to be fair to all people," he wrote in 1945, "and my selfish objective is to win baseball games."[26]

Commissioner Landis, who had been an ardent defender of the rights of minor leaguers, never acted with the same commitment when the subject of integration arose. Although he insisted there was no formal edict banning blacks from playing in the major leagues, he always upheld the status quo. His death in 1944 eliminated a final obstacle to Rickey's plan to integrate the game.

Rickey's strategy was to scout out the best black athlete for his purpose. He wanted someone who was strong enough to withstand the abuse he was sure to face. At the same time, he wanted an athlete who could perform up to major-league capabilities. He ordered his scouts to search for such a person, under the guise of looking for players to stock teams for a new black league that was forming.

After weeks of searching, Rickey found the player he was looking for. Jackie Robinson, a shortstop for the Kansas City Monarchs of the Negro American League, was one of the top athletes in the country. As a student at UCLA, he had starred in basketball, football, track, and swimming. Rickey signed him to a contract in 1945, assigning him to play for the Dodgers' Montreal farm team the next season. After being named the International League's Most Valuable Player, Robinson moved up to the Dodgers

When Jackie Robinson signed with the Dodgers, he became the first modern-day African American major league player.

FLEET WALKER

When Jackie Robinson broke baseball's color line in 1947, he became the first *modern* black man to play in the majors. The first black man actually played in a game nearly thirty-five years before Robinson was even born.

Moses Fleetwood Walker was a catcher with the Toledo Blue Stockings of the American Association in 1884, the circuit's third year of existence as a major league. A catcher by trade, Fleet, as he was known, batted .263 that year in forty-two games. Looking back at the obstacles he faced, it is amazing that he did even that well.

Although Walker proved popular with the fans, many of his Toledo teammates resented him. As reported in *The Ballplayers,* ace pitcher Tony Mullane once acknowledged that Walker "was the best catcher I ever worked with, but I disliked a Negro and whenever I had to pitch to him I used to pitch anything I wanted without looking at his signals." The young black, whose brother Welday also played in five games for Toledo that year, faced anonymous threats during the season but managed to play out the year. The Blue Stockings finished in eighth place, and folded following the end of the season.

Walker played several more seasons in the minors. In 1887, he teamed up with pitcher George Stovey on the Newark Little Giants of the International League to form organized baseball's first black battery. Later that year, the league formally announced its intention not to accept any more black players, and Walker's career came to an end. In later years, he published *Our Home Colony,* in which he concluded that the only solution to racial intolerance in America was for blacks to emigrate back to Africa.

in 1947. That April, he made history by becoming the first black to play in a major-league game in modern times. He went on to become the National League's Rookie of the Year that season. He championed the cause of the black man and won the admiration of people of all races. After a distinguished career in the majors, Robinson was elected to the Hall of Fame in 1962.

Despite Robinson's success, baseball was slow to integrate. The last of the sixteen major-league clubs to field a black player—the Boston Red Sox—did not do so until 1959. The first black manager, Frank Robinson, was not hired until 1975.

The "Great Experiment," as it was called, was still a success. Baseball had leaped to the forefront of the integration movement well before most other major social institutions. Segregation in the nation's schools, for example, would not be abolished until 1954. An era of baseball history had passed from the scene, and a new one was just around the corner.

The Postwar Era

Baseball's importance on the American scene was emphasized by President Franklin D. Roosevelt in 1942. With World War II in full swing, Roosevelt urged the major leagues to continue their regular schedule of games, citing the game's ability to boost American morale during troubled times. "I honestly feel that it would be best for the country to keep baseball going," said the president. "There will be fewer people unemployed and everybody will work longer hours and harder than ever before. And that means that they ought to have a chance for recreation and for taking their minds off their work even more than before."[27]

Dozens of major leaguers rushed off to join the service. They were replaced by an assortment of players who were far out of their league. Fifteen-year-old Joe Nuxhall made his debut with the Cincinnati Reds in 1944, while one-armed Pete Gray and one-legged Bert Shepard were also outfitted with uniforms. As Shepard admitted, "It's hard for a manager to realize that his best chance of winning is a guy with a leg off."[28]

When the war ended, baseball quickly returned to normal. "Normalcy" included a return to power of the Yankees. With most of their starters in the military, New York had dropped from its regular spot atop the American League standings in 1944. The St. Louis Browns won the pennant that year, the only time in their long history that they finished in first place.

In the National League, the Dodgers began to rise in the standings, driven by an influx of young black players. In addition to Robinson, Roy Campanella, Don Newcombe, Joe Black, Junior Gilliam, and several other African Americans would play key roles in future years. The two New York powers would meet in a "Subway" World Series a total of six times in the ten-year period beginning in 1947.

The years following the end of World War II saw the country go through a number of significant changes. People began moving out of the big cities and into the suburbs, as peacetime brought with it a boost to the nation's economy. With more jobs available, and more money to be made, more was spent on leisure activities.

The baseball scene reflected these changes in the American lifestyle. Attendance increased as people took the time to enjoy their hobbies and other interests. Owners began thinking about relocating franchises to new population centers, keenly aware of the opportunity for increased revenues. The Braves moved from Boston to Milwaukee in 1953, the first such franchise shift in more than fifty years. It was followed in short order by four other moves: the Browns from St. Louis to Baltimore in 1954; the Athletics from Philadelphia to Kansas City in 1955; and the Dodgers and Giants from Brooklyn and New York to Los Angeles and San Francisco, respectively, after the 1957 season.

Interest in baseball was further spurred by the revolution brought about by television. Income from television increased the value of major-league franchises, allowing fans to watch their teams even if they could not make it to the ballpark. Stars such as Willie Mays, Mickey Mantle, Ted Williams, Stan Musial, Bob Feller, and Warren Spahn could be seen by fans who lived where no major-league franchise existed.

With television, fans could see stars such as Ted Williams (left), Stan Musial (center), and Willie Mays (right) without traveling to the ballpark.

The other side of the coin, however, was that the small screen introduced many fans to other sports, like professional football and basketball. Baseball was no longer the only game in town, and attendance began to level off in the 1950s.

The increased revenue filling team coffers had another even more significant effect. Reflecting a trend which had grown in the American workplace, players began to organize themselves in order to reap more benefits from the owners. In 1946, they formed the American Baseball Guild under the direction of attorney Robert Murphy. When threatened with the possibility of a strike, the owners agreed to establish a minimum salary and a pension plan to be funded with the increased television revenues.

The Guild did not last long, but when owners attempted to cancel the pension plan, the players fought back by forming the Major League Baseball Players Association. The Players Association helped the

THE MEXICAN LEAGUE

In 1946, millionaire Jorge Pasquel and his four brothers attempted to lure several major leaguers to play south of the border in the Mexican League. Some, like St. Louis Cardinals star Stan Musial, refused substantial salary offers. Others, including Vern Stephens, Max Lanier, Sal Maglie, Mickey Owen, Lou Klein, Fred Martin, and Danny Gardella, did not. Former Kentucky governor A. B. "Happy" Chandler, who had been elected baseball's second commissioner upon Judge Landis's death, took a firm stance against the jumpers. He announced they would be banished from organized baseball, following the precedent set by Landis in previous years.

Within time, most of the jumpers grew disenchanted with playing conditions in Mexico and tried to rejoin their American teams. The owners, however, stood united in blacklisting them for five years. Rather than accept the ruling, Gardella filed a $300,000-dollar suit, claiming he had been bound by the reserve clause, and not a contract. Under threat of having the clause overturned, baseball agreed to settle the case out of court, paying Gardella $29,000, and lifting the suspension.

For the time being, the reserve clause remained intact. Future years, however, would see further challenges. These would eventually lead to the player free agency which has seen salaries skyrocket to unheard-of heights.

players retain the pension system and, more importantly, established itself as a force with which to be reckoned in the future.

Westward Ho

The Dodgers' and Giants' move to the West Coast in 1958 opened up a whole new region of the country to major-league baseball, with travel by airplane now being the norm. Other cities became enamored with the idea of having major-league teams to call their own. When William Shea and Branch Rickey unveiled plans for a new organization—the Continental League—to compete with the two existing leagues, major-league baseball agreed, instead, to place two new franchises in both the National and American Leagues. By 1962, the New York Mets and Houston Colt .45s had taken their place in the Senior Circuit. The Los Angeles Angels and Washington Senators (replacing the old Senators, who had relocated to Minnesota) had begun play in the American League the preceding season.

This first wave of expansion produced an important side effect. In 1965, the Houston club (now known as the Astros) opened in a new home stadium. The Astrodome, modestly called the "Eighth Wonder of the World," was baseball's first indoor stadium. The air-conditioned arena, built to counteract the city's stifling summer heat and humidity, produced its share of problems. Players could not see balls against the roof, so the ceiling panels had to be painted. This

The Astrodome, former home of the Houston Astros, was baseball's first indoor stadium.

solved one problem, but caused another. With sunlight now blocked, the grass on the field began to die.

The solution to this problem was the introduction of a new, artificial surface, called Astroturf. This new surface caused a significant change in the way the game was played, and was almost universally despised by players. Former Chicago White Sox infielder Richie Allen put it bluntly: "If horses don't eat it, I don't want to play on it."[29] Balls hit on the turf would either bounce high into the air or shoot through the infield like bullets. Infielders were forced to play back farther, and often bounced throws to first base since the surface gave true hops. Outfielders had to play deeper to prevent balls from shooting between them for extra-base hits.

Additionally, the hard undersurface of the turf caused a substantial number of turf-related injuries, especially to knees. As more new stadiums were built, many utilized artificial surfaces, making this an even more serious problem.

Despite generally poor performances by the expansion teams, and relatively modest gains in attendance, the majors expanded again in 1969. New franchises were planted in Kansas City and Seattle in the American League, and San Diego and Montreal in the National. With twelve teams now in each league, it was time for a change in postseason format. Each league was divided into two six-team divisions, with the winners meeting in a new round of playoffs to determine which teams would continue to the World Series.

Four races instead of two generated more interest among fans. New stadiums poured money into owners' pockets as luxury boxes rented for thousands of dollars a year. Lucrative television contracts further added to the cash flow. All this was not lost on the players, who began to question if they were getting their fair share of the profits.

Marvin Miller and the MLBPA

Until Marvin Miller was elected executive director of the Major League Baseball Players Association in 1966, the owners held the upper hand in all matters monetary. Under Judge Robert Cannon, the Players Association had made token gains in terms of an increased minimum salary for players and funding of a pension plan. The reserve clause was still in effect, however, binding players to a single team.

Miller came to the job after spending years in the field of labor-management relations with the International Association of Machinists, the United Automobile Workers, and the United Steel Workers of America. His deep-seated belief was that the players' services were worth far more than what the owners were paying them. He was determined to correct what he viewed as a one-sided arrangement. He quickly won the players' confidence and set out on a path that would make him, arguably, the most influential figure in baseball over the second half of the century.

Moving slowly at first, Miller was soon able to get management to sign a Basic Agreement which saw them agree to demands for collective bargaining, and which raised the minimum salary from seven thousand to ten thousand dollars. A threatened strike of spring-training camps in 1969 resulted in pension contributions being linked to increasing television revenues.

Three years later, the players, who had gradually become more and more unified behind Miller, walked out in the first general player strike in history, causing the cancellation of the first nine days of the regular season. This show of strength eventually

Marvin Miller won many victories for players.

led to the owners' acceptance of binding arbitration in matters of salary disputes with players who had two or more years of experience. No other ruling would contribute more to escalating player salaries.

It was during this period that St. Louis Cardinals outfielder Curt Flood made his historic attack on the reserve clause. Flood had been traded to the Philadelphia Phillies in October 1969, but refused to report. Instead, he sued baseball, contending that the clause violated federal antitrust laws. "I just didn't want to go to Philadelphia," he explained. "It was a selfish thing, really." [30]

Although the Supreme Court eventually ruled against Flood, the players, under Miller, became more united than ever in their determination to fight the reserve clause. When Jim "Catfish" Hunter was granted free agency in 1974 due to a contract violation by Oakland owner Charles Finley, the floodgates were opened. Hunter signed an incredible $3.75 million, five-year contract with the Yankees.

The next year, Miller won an even more important victory for the players. According to the standard player contract, if a player and team could not agree to terms,

"the Club shall have the right . . . to renew the contract for the period of one year on the same terms." [31] The clubs had always interpreted that as meaning contracts could be extended indefinitely, but Miller thought otherwise. He believed a player could become a free agent after playing one year without a contract. Pitchers Andy Messersmith and Dave McNally became Miller's test cases, as management dreaded the possible consequences. "If Messersmith wins his case," offered Dodgers manager Walter Alston, "baseball is dead." [32]

In December 1975, arbitrator Peter Seitz ruled in Messersmith's favor (McNally had decided to retire). The pitcher was declared a free agent, leaving the door open for every major leaguer to be declared likewise by simply playing in 1976 without signing a contract. Miller used this ruling as a bargaining chip in the next round of negotiations with the owners. He shrewdly offered a compromise by agreeing to limit free agency to players with six years of major-league service. For the first time in history, the players were no longer at the mercy of the owners when it came time for contract negotiations. A brand-new age was dawning.

CHAPTER 5

The Players Become Empowered

With the balance of power having shifted from the owners to the players, baseball took on a decidedly new complexion. Player salaries soared to previously undreamed-of heights as owners sought to improve their teams by signing free agents. The average annual salary in 1970 was just under $30,000. By 1975, it had risen to $45,000. Five years later, the average player was making $144,000 per year.

More Labor Problems

Management was becoming more and more concerned about finances. By 1980, the owners were looking to place a cap on the amounts which could be awarded through arbitration. Additionally, they hoped to establish a system of compensation whereby a team losing a free agent would receive players of equal value in return. In this way, they hoped to keep more aggressive owners from throwing ever-increasing amounts of money at available players. The players, of course, did not want to hear of this.

When a compromise could not be worked out, the owners announced the implementation of their own plan. In response, the players went on strike on June 12, 1981.

After seven weeks, the owners' united front began to crack. The strike was eventually settled when the players agreed to a form of limited compensation. The players a team might receive, however, were not of equal value to the ones lost. The end result was that there was no reason for bidding on free agents to stop.

Despite cries of poverty, the owners did not change their ways. Players became wealthier and, thus, more susceptible to illegal temptations. Rumors of drug abuse began to surface. St. Louis Cardinals manager Whitey Herzog estimated that approximately eleven players on his 1980 club were heavily into cocaine. Three years later, three members of the Kansas City Royals received prison sentences for attempting to purchase the drug.

When Commissioner Bowie Kuhn tried to institute a drug assistance program, the players resisted. It was not until 1984 that the players and owners agreed on a drug plan.

Collusion

Financial woes continued to haunt the teams. Eighteen of the twenty-six major-league clubs claimed to have lost money in 1984. Donald Fehr, who had taken over as the Major League Baseball Players Association executive director in 1983, disputed the assertion. In an effort to help curtail their own spending, the owners proposed several changes. They requested a salary

BASEBALL FAMILIES

Family plays an important role in the lives of Americans. In baseball, families have been represented dating all the way back to the Wright brothers, George and Harry, at the birth of the National League. Since then, approximately 350 brother combinations have seen action in the major leagues.

The most prolific combination, in terms of the number of siblings, was the Delahantys. Five brothers played in the majors, led by Hall of Famer Ed Delahanty. Joe, Jim, Frank, and Tom were the others to make the big time from the Cleveland-born clan.

Several families have had three brothers make the grade. The DiMaggios (Joe, Dom, and Vince), Boyers (Ken, Clete, and Cloyd), and Alous (Felipe, Matty, and Jesus) are among the most prominent. Brother pairs of note include the Waners (Paul and Lloyd), who, along with the Wrights, both made the Hall of Fame. Other significant achievements by brother duos include winning batting championships (Harry and Dixie Walker), finishing first and second in a batting race (Matty and Felipe Alou in 1966), and winning twenty games in the same season (Jim and Gaylord Perry in 1970, and Joe and Phil Niekro in 1979).

Family acts have not been limited to siblings. Approximately 150 father-son sets have spent time on major-league rosters, with a couple of dads even managing their progeny. The first father-son-grandson combination to make the grade was the Boones (father Ray, son Bob, and grandsons Bret and Aaron).

Perhaps the most significant performance achieved by a father and son was accomplished by Ken Griffey Sr. and Jr. The two Griffeys played in the same Seattle Mariners outfield in 1990. On September 14 of that year, the pair hit back-to-back home runs in the first inning of a 7-5 Seattle loss to the California Angels.

cap, limits to players eligible for arbitration, and limits to arbitration rewards. When no agreement could be reached, the players went on strike in August 1985. This walkout lasted only two days. Commissioner Peter Ueberroth, who had replaced Kuhn the previous year, got both sides to agree to a compromise, and an uneasy truce prevailed.

The owners, however, had formulated their own strategy. Beginning after the end of the 1985 season, players who were free agents mysteriously found few teams interested in their services. Many were forced to re-sign with their old teams for far less than what they should have commanded on the open market.

To the players, it seemed obvious that the owners had made an agreement amongst themselves in an effort to stop salaries from escalating. The owners denied this. "[It's] not a conspiracy," explained Commissioner Ueberroth, "it's common sense. The pot is dry."[33]

Two arbitrators eventually sided with the players. The owners were found guilty of collusion and ordered to pay $280 million in compensation. Salaries continued to spiral upward. When the 1991 season began, nearly a third of all major leaguers were earning at least $1 million per year.

By then, many fans had become disillusioned with the players. Free agency, long-term contracts, player agents, renegotiations, and strikes had taken their toll. Newspaper sports pages were reading more and more like financial sections, with money issues filling the headlines more often than not.

Parity

Despite increasing salaries, baseball continued to prosper. Television money poured into league and team coffers in record amounts. Ueberroth negotiated a $1.08 billion, four-year deal with CBS in the early 1990s and obtained additional revenues from ESPN. Income from local media outlets added considerably to the value of big-market teams like the Yankees.

Predictions that free agency would lead to baseball's downfall proved to be unfounded. Since players were not eligible to reap the benefits until they had six years of major-league service, free agents were often past their prime playing years. The wealthier teams did not automatically win year after year. Surprisingly, the years following free agency saw more teams, rather than fewer, win divisional titles and pennants. From 1980 through 1990, only Cleveland, Texas, and Seattle of the twenty-six major-league franchises did not see any postseason action.

Another factor contributing to parity was the amateur draft. Instituted in 1965, the draft became the process by which all top high school and college prospects were selected. Teams drafted in the reverse order of their finish in the previous season's standings. Players could either sign with the team that selected them, or wait six months to be drafted again. No longer were the richest teams able to sign the cream of the amateur crop.

Baseball was strong enough to prosper even while suffering through a series of unfortunate incidents. The year 1989, in particular, saw the sport reel from one blow after another.

The biggest story of the year was Pete Rose's implication in a gambling scandal. In August, recently appointed commissioner Bart Giamatti imposed a lifetime ban on the all-time hits leader because of what was said to be overwhelming evidence that Rose had bet on baseball games while managing the Cincinnati Reds. As far as the scandal's effect on baseball, Giamatti said, "Let no one think it did not hurt baseball. That hurt will pass, however,

Pete Rose was banned from baseball for life for betting on games while managing the Cincinnati Reds.

as the great glory of the game asserts itself and a resilient institution goes forward. Let it also be clear that no individual is superior to the game."[34] Ever since the Black Sox scandal, baseball had been especially attentive to any suggestions that the integrity of the game might be compromised in any way. In a tragic follow-up, the fifty-one-year-old Giamatti died of a heart attack eight days after issuing his ban.

Another jolt to the game came during baseball's ultimate showcase, the World Series. A half hour before the San Francisco Giants were to meet the Oakland Athletics in Game 3 on October 17, an earthquake struck the San Francisco bay area. Damage to Candlestick Park and the surrounding area caused the Series to be delayed for ten days.

As it had done in the past, however, baseball was able to bounce back once again. Despite the high costs involved in running a major-league franchise, there was no shortage of buyers looking to become members of the owners' fraternity. When the Baltimore Orioles were put up for auction in 1993, they attracted a record sale price of $173 million.

The 1994 season began on a promising note. The dedication of two new ballparks all but guaranteed that new attendance marks would be set in both Cleveland and Texas.

THE GIRLS OF SUMMER

Although baseball has been a predominantly male pastime over the years, women have also played a role in its history. Among the earliest participants were those who played on teams at women's colleges, such as Vassar, before the turn of the century. Other notable females included Alta Weiss, who pitched for an all-male semipro team in 1907, and Jackie Mitchell, who was the first woman to sign a professional contract, doing so with the Class AA Chattanooga Lookouts in 1931. Mitchell's main claim to fame was striking out Babe Ruth and Lou Gehrig in an exhibition game against the New York Yankees that spring. Women were officially banned from signing with men's teams in 1952, shortly after Harrisburg of the Interstate League signed Eleanor Engle as a publicity stunt.

The most famous women players of all were those of the All-American Girls Professional Baseball League (AAGPBL). The league, first organized as a softball league by Chicago Cubs owner Philip K. Wrigley during World War II, was memorialized in the feature film *A League of Their Own* . Debuting in 1943 with four teams (the Kenosha Comets, Racine Belles, Rockford Peaches, and South Bend Blue Sox), the league was a showcase for many of the top female athletes of the day. Nearly six hundred women performed in the league during its twelve years of existence. The quality of play and level of competition earned the AAGPBL many fans. Attendance increased in each of its first six seasons, reaching a high in 1948, when the league's ten clubs attracted more than nine hundred thousand fans.

In 1994, the Colorado Silver Bullets became the first professional women's team since the AAGPBL. The squad barnstormed across the country, playing games against men's college, semipro, and minor-league teams. Another significant event came four years later when Ila Borders, a pitcher with the independent minor-league Duluth Dukes, became the first woman to defeat a men's team in a professional game.

Today, girls compete with boys on Little League teams across the nation. Although many barriers have been broken, however, it appears unlikely that a woman will grace the roster of a major-league team anytime in the near future.

Pitcher Jackie Mitchell, who struck out Babe Ruth and Lou Gehrig.

AN ALL-AMERICAN FAVORITE

There is probably no food that is more all-American than the hot dog. And, certainly, there is none more closely associated with the game of baseball. An automobile manufacturer joined the two together several years ago, using a jingle that shouted the praises of "Baseball, hot dogs, apple pie, and Chevrolet."

Although food and drink have been available at concession stands at ballparks dating back to at least 1875, the man who became the first concession magnate was Harry M. Stevens. Stevens began in the business by selling programs to fans, imploring them to buy his wares by explaining, "You can't tell the players without a scorecard."

Stevens soon expanded his enterprise to include selling foods, among which was the popular frankfurter, or "dachshund sausage," as it was known in New York. Vendors hawked these "red hots" on a bun to hungry fans at the Polo Grounds around the turn of the century. Thomas "Tad" Dorgan captured the essence of the scene in a cartoon for the *New York Evening Journal.* Instead of the vendor's cry of, "Get your red hot dachshunds!" he shortened it to "Hot dogs!" in the caption. Some suggested his change was due to his inability to spell "dachshunds."

Baseball food has changed with the years, and hungry fans can now find everything from crab cakes to sushi at ballparks across the country. Despite stiff competition from new favorites like pizza and nachos, the first food of choice among fans remains the same. Whether served plain, or slathered with mustard, relish, ketchup, or sauerkraut, the simple hot dog is still number one.

The National League had added two new franchises the previous year—in Colorado and Florida—and both had been extremely successful at the gate. The Colorado Rockies had set a record by drawing nearly 4.5 million fans.

With the leagues now boasting a total of twenty-eight teams, a change in divisional alignment was put into effect. Each league grouped its teams into three, rather than two, divisions. This resulted in a third round of playoffs being added to postseason play. The second-place team with the best record in each league (called the "wild card" team) would join the three divisional champions in a round of games to determine the clubs that would meet in the League Championship Series. These two winners would then move on to the World Series.

Unfortunately, labor problems again loomed on the horizon. For many, this would be baseball's darkest moment of all.

The Strike

A cloud hanging over the beginning of the 1994 season was the lack of a basic agreement between the players and management. The owners were claiming, once again, to be on the brink of financial ruin. According to them, nineteen of the twenty-eight teams would lose money in 1994. With such dire prospects, the owners insisted that a salary cap was the only solution. Each team would then be limited in the amount that could be spent on salaries.

The players vehemently rejected this option. How could baseball be in such terrible financial shape, they argued, when the Orioles had just been sold for $173 million? How could the owners be losing money when they continued to throw larger and larger contracts at the prime free agents? As former pitcher Wayne Garland once said, "I didn't ask for the money, they offered it to me. No one was ever paid more than he was worth."[35]

The players worried that if no new agreement was reached by the end of the season, the owners would declare an impasse. Under federal law, they could then unilaterally impose their own economic plan for 1995, which would include a salary cap. The only leverage the players had was to strike sometime between the All-Star Game and the playoffs. This would hurt the owners the most. They would lose significant television money due them from a new national television contract which began with the All-Star Game.

The owners claimed to be united in their cause. Some predicted a long strike. "It has the potential to go into the '96 season,"[36] threatened White Sox owner Jerry Reinsdorf. On August 12, the players walked out. It was the eighth major-league baseball work stoppage in twenty-two years.

Despite meetings between the two sides, no progress was made. When September 9 arrived with no agreement in sight, acting commissioner Bud Selig announced that

the rest of the regular season, and the postseason, would be canceled. For the first time since 1905, no World Series would be played to conclude the season.

Unable to reach an agreement, the owners implemented their salary cap proposal on December 23. They began discussing plans for using replacement players for the 1995 season. January found President Bill Clinton entering the dispute. He ordered talks between the two sides to resume. Under pressure from the National Labor Relations Board, the owners soon scrapped their salary cap plan.

When spring training opened, replacement players took over for the regulars. Talks continued between the two sides, however, and some progress was made. Finally, in March, under pressure from the National Labor Relations Board, the owners offered to continue under the salary arbitration and free-agent system which had been in effect previously. The players accepted. After seven and a half months, the longest strike in professional sports history was over. The total losses amounted to 921 regular season games and more than $800 million in lost revenue.

The Long Road Back

Although a truce had been reached, it would be a while before a new Basic Agreement could be worked out. That would take place in November 1996. Among other things, the players agreed to a luxury tax on salaries,

Many fans felt betrayed when baseball players went on strike during the 1994 season.

and the owners gave up the idea of a salary cap. They also allowed players major-league service time for regular season days lost by the strike. The new agreement, which would run through October 31, 2000, was something both sides could live with. "When you look at all the alternatives," said Arizona Diamondbacks owner Jerry Colangelo, "whether you like all the parts or not, it was the right thing to do."[37]

In the meantime, however, work needed to be done to win back the fans. This was not lost on the players. "It might take fans a little while to get over their crushed feelings," said Detroit second baseman Lou Whitaker. "It's just like a man and a woman. Maybe we'll send a few flowers."[38]

It did, indeed, take time for things to return to the way they were prior to the strike. Fans organized boycotts and attendance

64

dropped, along with television ratings. The 1995 season, however, found fans willing to forgive and forget. Sparked by the first full schedule of games in three years, attendance picked up significantly. An unprecedented surge in home-run hitting also helped. A record eighty-two players hit twenty or more homers in 1996, with fourteen stroking forty or more. This, however, was only a preview of things to come.

In 1998 and 1999, Mark McGwire of the St. Louis Cardinals and Sammy Sosa of the Chicago Cubs captivated fans all across the nation with their unprecedented home-run barrage. In 1998, McGwire shattered Roger Maris's thirty-seven-year-old season mark by hitting an incredible seventy round-trippers. Unbelievably, Sosa also surpassed the old record by smacking sixty-six him-

self. The following year, both again topped sixty homers, with McGwire stroking sixty-five and Sosa sixty-three.

Meanwhile, in the American League, the New York Yankees were reasserting themselves as baseball's best team. In 1998, they won a record 125 games for the season, including a 4-game sweep of the Padres in the World Series. Although not quite so dominating in 1999, the New Yorkers still managed to win their second consecutive world title, this time sweeping the Atlanta Braves.

The fans' response to the excitement of the last years of the century was positive. Millions followed Cal Ripken Jr.'s every move as he shattered Lou Gehrig's "unbreakable" mark of 2,130 consecutive games played. He eventually reached 2,632 before benching himself in late 1998. (Ripken's

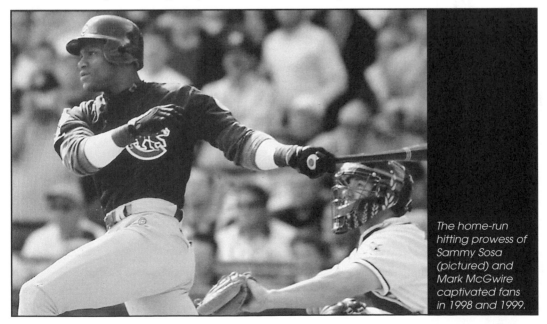

The home-run hitting prowess of Sammy Sosa (pictured) and Mark McGwire captivated fans in 1998 and 1999.

explanation for his longevity was simple. "When I came up in 1981," said Cal, "I sat in the dugout for the first time and watched. I said to myself, 'If I ever get a chance to play, I'm never coming out.'")[39]

The sport added two new franchises in 1998, with the Tampa Bay Devil Rays joining the American League and the Arizona Diamondbacks the National. The new playoff format proved to be a success, as did interleague play.

A whole new generation of ballplayers stood ready to carry on in the tradition of the greats who came before them. The baton had been passed, from Cobb and Ruth, to DiMaggio and Williams, to Mantle and Mays, and now to Griffey and McGwire. It appeared that rumors of baseball's death were greatly exaggerated. As Commissioner Bud Selig said, "Baseball heads for the 21st century more popular than it's ever been."[40]

CHAPTER 6

The Best of the Best

Hitting a baseball is arguably the single most difficult skill to master in all of sports. It is one of several talents that a player must possess in order to excel in the major leagues.

When baseball scouts evaluate prospects, they generally look for five basic skills—hitting for average, hitting for power, fielding, running, and throwing. Over the years, the players who have set the standards that others aim for have excelled in several or all of these categories.

Ty Cobb

Ty Cobb is remembered as baseball's fiercest competitor. He was also the game's most despised player.

As a hitter, Cobb had no peer. His lifetime batting average of .367 is the highest of all time. Until surpassed by Pete Rose in 1985, his career total of 4,191 hits was unmatched. Cobb's twelve American League batting titles, including nine in a row, is another major-league mark, as is his standard of 2,246 runs scored. His name can also be found in the top five on the all-time listings for doubles, triples, total bases, runs batted in, and stolen bases.

Cobb, who would do anything necessary to win, was vilified for his combativeness. Opposing infielders would cringe when they saw him sharpening his spikes in the dugout before a game. They knew their bodies would suffer the consequences if they dared stand between him and the base he desired to reach.

Ty Cobb, known for his aggressive style of play, holds the highest career batting average of all time.

a time, suspected that his wife was having an affair. In order to catch her in the act, he pretended to leave on one of his trips, then returned to their house later that night. Thinking he was a burglar, Ty's mother shot and killed him. Although Mrs. Cobb was exonerated, many in the town felt the incident was not an accident. The memory of the incident remained with the young Cobb for the rest of his life.

Pete Rose

No player in history ever played more games (3,562), batted more times (14,053), or got more hits (4,256) than Peter Edward Rose. He was an important cog in Cincinnati's "Big Red Machine" of the 1970s. His all-out style of play, which included headfirst slides and running out bases on balls, brought him legions of admirers. During his career, he played for six pennant winners and three world champions (two with the Reds and one with the Phillies), while compiling a lifetime batting average of .303. As a local hero, he later managed Cincinnati for six seasons.

If physical attacks did not have the desired effect, Cobb was not beneath using verbal ones. He had a reputation as a racist and would often insult an opponent's heritage in an attempt to make him lose control.

Many have attributed Cobb's ruthlessness to a tragic incident which occurred just prior to his call to the majors in 1905. Cobb's father, whose business affairs often kept him away from home for days at

Unfortunately, Rose's combativeness and brashness could also rub people the wrong way. He reportedly lost hundreds of thousands of dollars betting but refused to admit that he had a problem. In 1989, he was suspended from baseball for life by commissioner Bart Giamatti because of his involvement in gambling. The next year, he was found guilty of tax evasion and sentenced to several months in prison. Because of the evidence that he bet on baseball games, he was barred from entry into the Hall of Fame. Unfortunately, "Charlie Hustle's" contributions to the game of baseball between the white lines were diminished by his indiscretions off the field.

Ted Williams

Ted Williams once said, "All I want out of life is that when I walk down the street, folks will say, 'There goes the greatest hit-ter who ever lived.'"[41] Many believe he reached that goal.

Williams stands tied for sixth on the all-time list of batting leaders with an average of .344, second in slugging percentage with a .634 mark, and tied for tenth in home runs with 521. His record would have been even more impressive had he not lost five full seasons of his career to military service in World War II and the Korean War.

The "Splendid Splinter" won six batting titles and two Triple Crowns. He is the last player to bat .400 for a season, compiling a .406 mark in 1941. In 1958 he became the oldest player to win a title, doing so at age forty. Williams won the

Ted Williams, who hit .406 in 1941, is the last player to bat over .400 for a season.

American League Most Valuable Player award in both 1946 and 1949, and could well have won three more had he had a better relationship with the press. Unfortunately, his arrogance and disdain for the media cost him votes when election time came around.

When his playing days were over, Williams took over as manager of the Texas Rangers. He won the American League Manager of the Year award in 1969 when he led Texas to a twenty-one-game improvement over the team's record of the previous year.

Babe Ruth

Any discussion of power hitters must begin with Babe Ruth, the most famous player in baseball history. As Hall of Fame pitcher Walter Johnson once said, "He can hit any kind of ball that ever came within his reach hard enough to split the cover."[42] Even today, with his two most famous records having been broken, he is still considered the greatest home-run hitter of all time.

After beginning his career as a pitcher, Ruth was switched to the outfield so that his bat would be in the lineup every day. At the age of twenty-four, he slugged 29 home runs for the Red Sox to set a new single-season mark. Two years later, he became the sport's all-time career leader, passing Roger Connor's total of 138 home runs set prior to the turn of the century. He

held the lifetime record for fifty-three years, until Hank Aaron passed him in 1974. Aaron's total of 755 is 41 ahead of the Bambino's 714.

Just as Ruth's career mark has fallen, so too has his single-season standard. His record of 60 home runs, set in 1927, lasted thirty-four years until Roger Maris belted 61 in 1961.

Stories about the Babe abound, ranging from his called home run in the 1932 World Series against the Cubs to the infamous stomach ache which kept him out for much of the 1925 season. His excesses were legendary, as was his love for kids.

The Babe saved baseball after the Black Sox Scandal of 1919. His exploits on the diamond spurred an increase in attendance. They also helped raise the salary scale for players everywhere. As former teammate Waite Hoyt said, "Every big league player and his wife should teach their children to pray: 'God bless Mommy, God bless Daddy, and God bless Babe Ruth.'"[43]

Hank Aaron

When Hank Aaron was closing in on baseball's all-time home run mark in 1973, he found himself haunted by more than just the ghost of Babe Ruth. Aaron received hundreds of letters threatening him with bodily harm if he had the audacity to surpass the mark held by the beloved Bambino. Things got so bad that he was eventually assigned a bodyguard by the Atlanta Police Department. Aaron ultimately prevailed, and the record fell on April 8, 1974, as he hit career home-run number 715 off Al Downing of the Los Angeles Dodgers.

Aaron began his twenty-three-year sojourn in the big leagues as a second baseman with the Milwaukee Braves. He went about his job with quiet dignity, rarely receiving the attention given to his peers, like Willie Mays and Roberto Clemente. His career was a model of sustained consistency. Aaron batted over .300 fourteen times, hit 20 or more home runs in twenty consecutive seasons, and drove home more than 100 runs fifteen times, including a record thirteen years in a row.

Hammerin' Hank had a low-key approach to the game, exemplified by his style of batting. Hall of Fame pitcher Robin Roberts once said that Aaron "could fall asleep between pitches and still wake up in time to hit the next one."[44]

Mark McGwire powered his way into the record books by launching seventy home runs in 1998.

Mark McGwire

The year 1998 saw Mark McGwire break one of baseball's longest-standing records. It had been thirty-seven years since Roger Maris broke Babe Ruth's mark of 60 home runs in a season by hitting 61 in 1961. In 1998, not only did McGwire demolish the mark by hitting an incredible 70 home runs, Sammy Sosa of the Cubs also broke the old standard, falling four short of McGwire by clouting 66. The next year, the pair duplicated the feat. McGwire belted 65 in 1999 and Sosa, 63.

The red-headed McGwire gave early notice of his power by hitting a rookie record of 49 home runs for the Oakland Athletics in 1987. It was not until he came over to the St. Louis Cardinals, however, that he hit his stride. Beginning in 1996, he surpassed the 50-home-run mark a record four years in a row, averaging an unbelievable 61.25 round-trippers per season.

JOE BAUMAN, HOME RUN KING

When Mark McGwire and Sammy Sosa were chasing the major-league home run mark in 1998, media coverage was overwhelming. Newspapers and television stations across the country reported their every move to an anxious public.

The scenario was quite a bit different back in 1954. That was the year that thirty-two-year-old Joe Bauman of the Roswell Rockets in the Class C Longhorn League set the all-time professional home-run standard by clouting 72 four-baggers. No one has ever hit more.

Bauman was a six-foot, five-inch, 245-pound first baseman. He never spent a day in the majors. In 1954, however, he had a season to be remembered. In addition to his 72 homers, Bauman had 199 hits, batted .398, drove home 224 runs, walked 150 times, collected 456 total bases, and recorded a slugging percentage of .916. Incredibly, he did all this while playing just 138 games. (That pace works out to 85 homers for a 162-game schedule.)

Of course, this was not the major leagues. Park Field, the Rockets' home, was located 3,573 feet above sea level, so the ball carried well in the thin atmosphere. Still, no one at any level of professional ball has ever attained such a lofty mark. The previous record was 69 home runs in a sea-

Joe Bauman holds the minor league record for home runs with seventy-two.

son, reached by Joe Hauser of the Double A Minneapolis Millers of the American Association in 1933, and by Bob Crues of the Amarillo Gold Sox of the Class C West Texas–New Mexico League in 1948.

Unfortunately, McGwire's heroics have been tainted in the eyes of some by his use of the dietary supplement androstenedione. Researchers have found that "andro" raises testosterone above normal levels and could enhance athletic performance. Although the supplement is banned by the Olympics, the NCAA, and the National Football League, it is not prohibited by major-league baseball.

Rickey Henderson

Few people in baseball circles would argue with the statement that Rickey Henderson is the greatest leadoff hitter of all time, as well as the game's greatest base stealer. His distinctive combination of speed and power ensure his admission into the Baseball Hall of Fame in Cooperstown when his playing days are over.

As a twenty-year-old rookie in 1979, the Oakland outfielder stole 33 bases. The next year he pilfered exactly 100, giving him the first of his twelve titles. He would surpass the century mark in two of the next three seasons, setting a new major-league record in 1982 with an astonishing 130. Henderson moved into first place on the all-time list in 1991, and has continued to add to his total. By 2000, he had stolen 1,334 bases, or nearly 400 more than runner-up Lou Brock.

Possessing unusual power for a leadoff hitter, Henderson has swatted close to 300 home runs in his career, and driven in more than 1,000 runs. He is one of only six players to score more than 2,000 runs, and trails only Babe Ruth and Ted Williams in total walks. Henderson also holds the major-league record for home runs leading off a ball game.

The Oakland outfielder broke Brock's record for career stolen bases when he pilfered number 939 on May 1, 1991. The record was not the top baseball story of the day, however. Nolan Ryan picked that same night to pitch his record-setting seventh career no-hitter.

Maury Wills

After a long hiatus, speed came into fashion once again in the mid-1950s. Luis Aparicio began a record string of eight consecutive American League stolen base crowns in 1956. In the National League, Dodger shortstop Maury Wills won the first of six consecutive titles in 1960. Two years later, he eclipsed Ty Cobb's record and became the first modern player to steal 100 bases in a season. He finished the year with 104. His daring on the base paths gave opposing managers fits. "My instructions for preventing Wills from stealing are simple," explained Cincinnati manager Fred Hutchinson sarcastically. "Don't let him get on base."[45]

In his prime, Wills proved that speed, when combined with pitching, could be a lethal combination. He sparked the punchless Dodgers to four pennants and three world championships in his years with the team. His speed helped manufacture runs as Sandy Koufax, Don Drysdale, and company kept the opposition in check. Wills's importance to his team was confirmed by the baseball writers who voted him the National League Most Valuable Player in 1962.

Willie Mays

Many baseball experts consider Willie Mays to be the greatest all-around player the game of baseball has ever seen. He ranks third on the career home-run list with 660, and also makes the Top Ten in games (seventh), runs scored (sixth), hits (tenth), total bases (third), extra-base hits (fourth), and runs batted in (eighth).

Willie Mays was one of the greatest hitters of all time but he is best known for his superb defensive skills.

On defense, Mays was arguably the most exciting outfielder ever to don a glove. His ability to track down fly balls and put them away with his patented basket catch foiled many a rally. Mets manager Gil Hodges once explained his dilemma this way: "I can't very well tell my batters don't hit it to him. Wherever they hit it, he's there anyway."[46]

Mays won Gold Glove awards in each of the first twelve years they were given out. He is the author of what is probably the most famous catch in major-league history. In the 1954 World Series against the Cleveland Indians, the Giant center fielder caught Vic Wertz's 460-foot, eighth-inning drive, running full speed toward the wall in the Polo Grounds, with his back to home plate. After the catch, he spun around and rifled the ball back to the infield, preventing a run from scoring.

The Say-Hey Kid captivated New York fans with his exuberance and love for the game. The hat flying off his head as he raced after fly balls became his trademark. Mays was a one-of-a-kind player who thrilled everyone who had the privilege of seeing him play.

Brooks Robinson

In 1957, the Rawlings Sporting Goods firm came up with the idea of presenting awards to the best fielders at each position. They called the awards the Gold Gloves. No one has ever won more Gold Gloves than Baltimore Orioles third baseman Brooks Robinson, the "Human Vacuum Cleaner."

By the time he retired, Robinson held every career fielding mark for third baseman—assists, putouts, double plays, and fielding percentage. His standing as an all-time fielding great was solidified by his remarkable performance in the 1970 World Series. Time and time again, he robbed Cincinnati Reds batters of potential hits. It got so bad that Cincinnati slugger Johnny Bench moaned, "I will become a lefthanded hitter to keep the ball away from that guy."[47] Robinson fully realized the significance of his play. "I don't think there's any

Brooks Robinson was dubbed the "Human Vacuum Cleaner" because of his stellar defensive play.

doubt," he said, "that the Series helped establish me as a fielder and was a springboard for getting me into the Hall of Fame."[48]

Robinson's artistry with the glove caused many people to overlook his offensive skills. He clouted 268 home runs in his career, while compiling a lifetime batting average of .267. In 1964 he won the American League Most Valuable Player award, with 28 homers, 118 runs batted in, and a batting mark of .317.

Cy Young

Cy Young set records in his twenty-two-year career as a pitcher that will almost certainly never be equaled. Pitching mainly for the Cleveland Spiders of the National League and Boston of the American League around the turn of the century, he ate up innings in record numbers. He hurled a total of 7,356 frames, while no other pitcher has even reached 6,000. He also threw 749 complete games for another major league mark.

Young's final ledger shows 511 victories, an incredible 94 more than his nearest challenger, Walter Johnson. On the other side, however, are 316 losses, also a career record. Young won 30 or more games in a season five times, and 20 or more games on ten other occasions. He hurled three no-hitters, including a perfect game. His most amazing feat was that of tossing 24 consecutive hitless innings over the course of three games (including the perfect game) in May 1904.

Young was elected to baseball's Hall of Fame in 1937. In recognition of his many accomplishments, baseball established the Cy Young Award in 1956. It is presented annually to the best pitcher in each league.

Satchel Paige

It is hard to distinguish where reality leaves off and legend begins with Leroy "Satchel" Paige. In a career that spanned forty years (mostly in the Negro Leagues and with barnstorming teams), Paige appeared in some 2,500 games, winning 2,000, including 100 no-hitters. He regularly pitched against All-Star teams made up of white major leaguers, winning more often than he lost. Many big leaguers, including Dizzy Dean, Charlie Gehringer, and Joe DiMaggio, called the skinny right-hander the best pitcher they had ever faced.

According to those who played with him, Paige would occasionally call in his outfielders, then proceed to strike out the side. Stories such as this ensured large crowds wherever he pitched (whether or not the stories were accurate). A true showman, Paige named each of his pitches. His famous hesitation pitch (where he would pause just as his forward foot hit the ground) would tie batters up in knots.

In 1948, Bill Veeck brought Paige to the majors. Probably forty-two years old at the time, Paige compiled a 6-1 record with a

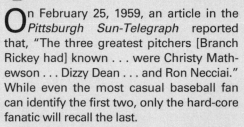

RON NECCIAI, AN IMPROBABLE RECORD

On February 25, 1959, an article in the *Pittsburgh Sun-Telegraph* reported that, "The three greatest pitchers [Branch Rickey had] known . . . were Christy Mathewson . . . Dizzy Dean . . . and Ron Necciai." While even the most casual baseball fan can identify the first two, only the hard-core fanatic will recall the last.

Necciai was a nineteen-year-old pitcher in the Pittsburgh Pirates organization. When he took the mound for the Bristol Twins of the Class D Appalachian League on May 13, 1952, he was known as much for his jittery stomach (the result of an ulcer) as he was for his pitching. That night, however, he achieved what the National Association of Professional Baseball Leagues later recognized as the most famous record in minor-league baseball.

Necciai was a hard-throwing, skinny right-hander who had originally signed as a first baseman. He switched to the mound early in his career, but experienced little success until he came under the tutelage of Bristol manager George Detore. When

he took the mound that night, he put everything together. He no-hit the Welch Miners, winning by a score of 7-0. He allowed one walk in the contest, and hit one batter. The reason the 1,183 fans in attendance would always remember the game, however, was for something else he did. In the nine-inning contest, Necciai struck out the amazing total of twenty-seven batters. The only balls the Miners hit into fair territory were two grounders to the Bristol shortstop. The first was handled cleanly, and the second was booted for an error.

With two outs in the ninth inning, a third strike got past the Bristol catcher. The batter reached first base safely, even though he was recorded as the twenty-sixth strike out victim. Necciai proceeded to fan the next hitter to complete his gem. Only one other hurler ever struck out as many as twenty-five batters in a professional game. In his very next start for Bristol, Necciai fanned twenty-four, giving him an amazing two-game total of fifty-one strikeouts.

2.48 earned run average as the Indians won the American League pennant. His brief major-league career saw him record a 28-31 mark, with a 3.29 ERA and 32 saves. In 1965, Charles Finley brought him back to pitch in one game for the Oakland Athletics. At age fifty-nine, Paige hurled three scoreless innings of one-hit ball against the Boston Red Sox, adding to the legend.

Paige was known for his homespun philosophy. His six steps for eternal youth included such sound advice as "Avoid fried meats, which angry up the blood," and "Don't look back. Something might be gaining on you."[49] In 1972, Paige became the first of the Negro-league stars admitted to the Hall of Fame.

Nolan Ryan

The emphasis placed on the home run in the modern-day game has had an important side effect. Strikeout totals have soared, with players swinging from the heels rather than concentrating on just making contact. One pitcher with claims to being the hardest thrower of all time is Hall of Famer Nolan Ryan. In twenty-seven major league seasons, Ryan fanned a total of 5,714 batters. Left-hander Steve Carlton, with 4,136, is the only pitcher within 2,000 strikeouts of him.

Nolan Ryan overwhelmed hitters with his fastball en route to his single-season record 383 strikeouts in 1973.

Ryan also holds the single-season record. He fanned 383 batters in 1973, surpassing Sandy Koufax's previous standard by a single strikeout. Pitchers have fanned 300 in a season only twenty-two times, with Ryan having performed the feat on five occasions.

Another record not likely to be broken anytime soon is that for most no-hitters. The lefty Koufax hurled no-hitters in four consecutive seasons for the Dodgers, from 1962 to 1965. The mark lasted until Ryan came on the scene. Ryan tossed two hitless games for the California Angels in 1973, then followed up with others in 1974 and 1975. He moved on to Houston, where he hurled his record-breaking fifth in 1981. Coming back to the American League, Ryan pitched a sixth no-hitter for Texas in 1990, and an incredible seventh for the Rangers the next year at age forty-four. In addition to these gems, Ryan also tossed twelve one-hitters in his career.

Casey Stengel

A solid hitter during his days as an active player, Casey Stengel made the Hall of Fame because of his achievements as a manager. After several less-than-

STEVE DALKOWSKI, THE FASTEST OF THEM ALL

Physical talent alone does not guarantee success on the ball field. If it did, a plaque bearing the likeness of Steven Louis Dalkowski would today grace the walls of baseball's Hall of Fame in Cooperstown. Dalkowski was arguably the fastest pitcher ever to throw a baseball. "I've umpired for Koufax, Gibson, Drysdale, Seaver, Maloney, Marichal and Gooden," related former big-league umpire Doug Harvey, "and they could all bring it, but nobody could bring it like Dalkowski." The problem with the young left-hander was that his wildness was as legendary as his speed.

Dalkowski looked like anything but the fastest pitcher ever. He stood five feet, nine inches tall and weighed 170 pounds soaking wet. With his glasses, he looked more like a schoolteacher than a professional athlete.

After graduating from high school, Dalkowski signed a four-thousand-dollar bonus contract with the Baltimore Orioles. Assigned to Kingsport in 1957 at the age of eighteen, he won just one game while losing eight. In 62 innings, however, he struck out an incredible 121 batters. Unfortunately, he walked an even more incredible 129. He bounced from one town to another in the Oriole system, never harnessing his amazing talent. One year, he tossed a no-hitter in which he struck out 24 batters and walked 18. He lost the game, 8-4. In the California League in 1960, he fanned 262 batters in 170 innings—and walked the same number.

The Orioles tried every way imaginable to help him control his fastball, but nothing seemed to work. Finally, in 1962 under manager Earl Weaver at Elmira, Dalkowski had the best season of his career. He began the next spring in fine fashion, and appeared likely to make the major-league club at last.

It was not meant to be, however. On March 23, 1963, in an exhibition game against the Yankees, Dalkowski threw a pitch and felt something pop in his elbow. He never had the same velocity again.

Dalkowski hung around the minors for two more years before finally hanging up his spikes. The fastest pitcher of them all ended his professional career with a record of forty-six wins and eighty losses, an earned run average of 5.59, and 1,354 walks and 1,396 strikeouts in 995 innings pitched. He never pitched a single inning in the majors.

---

successful years at the helm of the Dodgers and Braves, the "Old Perfesser" took over the reins of the Yankees in 1949. He guided the New Yorkers to a world championship that very first season, then proceeded to repeat the feat each of the next four years. He won ten pennants and seven championships all told, over a period of just twelve years.

Although Stengel was a shrewd manipulator of players, he is often thought of as a clownish figure, dating back to his days as a player. He once doffed his hat to the crowd, releasing a bird he had secreted underneath. Another time, he carried a flashlight onto the field with him to let the umpire know he thought it was too dark to continue playing.

Following his "retirement" from the Yankees ("I'll never make the mistake of being seventy again,"[50] he explained), he took the job as a manager of the expansion New York Mets. He promoted the team as no other person could, urging the fans to come out to see the "Amazins."

Stengel's unique version of the English language—known as Stengelese—confused and charmed fans and press alike. A blend of gibberish and double-talk, an example is inscribed on his tombstone. "There comes a time in every man's life," reads the inscription, "and I've had plenty of them."[51]

The Year 2000 and Beyond

Baseball's rules have not changed radically over the years. The way the game is played, however, has been transformed significantly.

The majority of today's fans seem to require fast action and high scoring in order to enjoy a sport. Baseball's laid-back, pastoral pace seems outdated to many. Some of the changes made to the game have been in an effort to win the approval of the modern fan.

Baseball today is a game of power, speed, and specialized pitching. Players are bigger and stronger than ever, in large part due to improvements in conditioning and nutrition. The new retro stadiums built in recent years generally have smaller dimensions, which results in more scoring. Artificial surfaces also help hitters, while assisting fielders as

well. Fewer bad bounces and truer hops mean higher fielding percentages. Fielders also use larger gloves than players of years past, allowing them to reach, and hold on to, more balls.

The increased usage and specialization of relief pitchers have made complete games a thing of the past. Relief pitchers are classified as middle relievers, setup men, and closers. Some hurlers reach one hundred miles per hour on the radar gun, while others mystify batters with new pitches like the split-fingered fastball and the knuckle curve. Hitters rarely face the same pitcher more than twice in a game, making it harder to achieve success.

The players themselves have also changed with the times. While baseball was

95 percent white a half century ago, today black and Hispanic players comprise approximately 30 percent of major-league rosters. Teams concentrate scouting efforts in Latin American countries, where baseball is played year-round. Towns like San Pedro de Macoris in the Dominican Republic have become baseball meccas. As former San Diego Padres general manager Joe McIlvaine said, "The talent in the Latin countries makes major league baseball what it is supposed to be—the best baseball in the world, and the best baseball players in the world. If there weren't Latin players, we couldn't say it's the best baseball in the world."[52] Other countries have also gotten into the act. The 1990s have seen players from Japan, Korea, and Australia make their presence felt in the majors.

The changing times have also brought problems with them, however. Higher salaries have been beneficial to the players but have hurt a number of franchises. As it now stands, small-market teams, realistically, have little chance of competing with major-market clubs. Fans in these smaller cities run the risk of losing their teams to municipalities offering owners new ballparks and other incentives to relocate.

The larger number of minority players have not been matched by a proportionate increase in front-office hirings. Since Frank Robinson became the first black manager in 1975, relatively few African Americans have joined that exclusive fraternity. Even

Frank Robinson, the first African American to manage a major league team.

fewer have made their way into management positions.

The competency and conduct of umpires have also raised questions. Out of shape, confrontational umps have put the men in blue in a bad light. Work stoppages have also caused them to lose support from the fans who pay their salaries. Centralizing umpires from both leagues under one office for the 2000 season is, hopefully, the first step toward rectifying some of these problems.

The future will certainly provide us with additional surprises. It is not beyond the realm of possibility that subsequent expansions may see teams placed in cities beyond

U.S. and Canadian borders, making future championship competitions true "World" Series. As in football, perhaps instant replay will find a place in the game. It is not hard to imagine a system utilizing lasers to call balls and strikes in an effort to make the umpires' job easier.

As unlikely as they may seem, these possibilities are certainly no wilder than the concepts of artificial turf, interleague play, and agents negotiating million-dollar contracts would have been to the fans of thirty years ago. The game will continue to grow and evolve, as must every institution that wishes to survive and thrive.

It is just as certain, however, that some things will remain the same. A new generation of superstars, led by Ken Griffey Jr., Alex Rodriguez, Mike Piazza, and Chipper Jones will win baseball new fans—who will cheer for the home team (be it New York or Tokyo) and boo the umpires (be they human or robotic). They will argue whether Babe Ruth was a greater home-run hitter than Mark McGwire, and they will continue to eat hot dogs at the ballpark.

As Hall of Fame catcher Roy Campanella once said, "To be good, you've gotta have a lot of little boy in you. When you see Willie Mays and Ted Williams jumping and hopping around the bases after hitting a home run, and the kissing and hugging that goes on at home plate, you realize they have to be little boys."[53] Baseball will always be played by little boys—no matter what their age.

Awards and Statistics

Most Valuable Player
(by year)

Position key
p: pitcher
c: catcher
1b: first base
2b: second base
3b: third base
ss: shortstop
of: outfield
(*) Unanimous selection

National League

1999	Chipper Jones, Atlanta, 3b
1998	Sammy Sosa, Chicago, of
1997	Larry Walker, Colorado, of
1996	*Ken Caminiti, San Diego, 3b
1995	Barry Larkin, Cincinnati, ss
1994	*Jeff Bagwell, Houston, 1b
1993	Barry Bonds, San Francisco, of
1992	Barry Bonds, Pittsburgh, of
1991	Terry Pendleton, Atlanta, 3b
1990	Barry Bonds, Pittsburgh, of
1989	Kevin Mitchell, San Francisco, of
1988	Kirk Gibson, Los Angeles, of
1987	Andre Dawson, Chicago, of
1986	Mike Schmidt, Philadelphia, 3b
1985	Willie McGee, St. Louis, of
1984	Ryne Sandberg, Chicago, 2b
1983	Dale Murphy, Atlanta, of
1982	Dale Murphy, Atlanta, of
1981	Mike Schmidt, Philadelphia, 3b
1980	*Mike Schmidt, Philadelphia, 3b
1979	(tie) Keith Hernandez, St. Louis, 1b;
	Willie Stargell, Pittsburgh, 1b
1978	Dave Parker, Pittsburgh, of
1977	George Foster, Cincinnati, of
1976	Joe Morgan, Cincinnati, 2b
1975	Joe Morgan, Cincinnati, 2b
1974	Steve Garvey, Los Angeles, 1b
1973	Pete Rose, Cincinnati, of
1972	Johnny Bench, Cincinnati, c
1971	Joe Torre, St. Louis, 3b
1970	Johnny Bench, Cincinnati, c
1969	Willie McCovey, San Francisco, 1b
1968	Bob Gibson, St. Louis, p
1967	*Orlando Cepeda, St. Louis, 1b
1966	Roberto Clemente, Pittsburgh, of
1965	Willie Mays, San Francisco, of
1964	Ken Boyer, St. Louis, 3b
1963	Sandy Koufax, Los Angeles, p
1962	Maury Wills, Los Angeles, ss
1961	Frank Robinson, Cincinnati, of
1960	Dick Groat, Pittsburgh, ss
1959	Ernie Banks, Chicago, ss
1958	Ernie Banks, Chicago, ss
1957	Hank Aaron, Milwaukee, of
1956	Don Newcombe, Brooklyn, p
1955	Roy Campanella, Brooklyn, c
1954	Willie Mays, New York, of
1953	Roy Campanella, Brooklyn, c
1952	Hank Sauer, Chicago, of
1951	Roy Campanella, Brooklyn, c
1950	Jim Konstanty, Philadelphia, p
1949	Jackie Robinson, Brooklyn, 2b
1948	Stan Musial, St. Louis, of
1947	Bob Elliott, Boston, 3b
1946	Stan Musial, St. Louis, 1b
1945	Phil Cavarretta, Chicago, 1b
1944	Marty Marion, St. Louis, ss
1943	Stan Musial, St. Louis, of

1942	Mort Cooper, St. Louis, p		1964	Brooks Robinson, Baltimore, 3b
1941	Dolph Camilli, Brooklyn, 1b		1963	Elston Howard, New York, c
1940	Frank McCormick, Cincinnati, 1b		1962	Mickey Mantle, New York, of
1939	Bucky Walters, Cincinnati, p		1961	Roger Maris, New York, of
1938	Ernie Lombardi, Cincinnati, c		1960	Roger Maris, New York, of
1937	Joe Medwick, St. Louis, of		1959	Nellie Fox, Chicago, 2b
1936	Carl Hubbell, New York, p		1958	Jackie Jensen, Boston, of
1935	Gabby Hartnett, Chicago, c		1957	Mickey Mantle, New York, of
1934	Dizzy Dean, St. Louis, p		1956	*Mickey Mantle, New York, of
1933	Carl Hubbell, New York, p		1955	Yogi Berra, New York, c
1932	Chuck Klein, Philadelphia, of		1954	Yogi Berra, New York, c
1931	Frankie Frisch, St. Louis, 2b		1953	*Al Rosen, Cleveland, 3b
			1952	Bobby Shantz, Philadelphia, p

American League

1999	Ivan Rodriguez, Texas, c		1951	Yogi Berra, New York, c
1998	Juan Gonzalez, Texas, of		1950	Phil Rizzuto, New York, ss
1997	*Ken Griffey Jr., Seattle, of		1949	Ted Williams, Boston, of
1996	Juan Gonzalez, Texas, of		1948	Lou Boudreau, Cleveland, ss
1995	Mo Vaughn, Boston, 1b		1947	Joe DiMaggio, New York, of
1994	Frank Thomas, Chicago, 1b		1946	Ted Williams, Boston, of
1993	*Frank Thomas, Chicago, 1b		1945	Hal Newhouser, Detroit, p
1992	Dennis Eckersley, Oakland, p		1944	Hal Newhouser, Detroit, p
1991	Cal Ripken Jr., Baltimore, ss		1943	Spud Chandler, New York, p
1990	Rickey Henderson, Oakland, of		1942	Joe Gordon, New York, 2b
1989	Robin Yount, Milwaukee, of		1941	Joe DiMaggio, New York, of
1988	*Jose Canseco, Oakland, of		1940	Hank Greenberg, Detroit, of
1987	George Bell, Toronto, of		1939	Joe DiMaggio, New York, of
1986	Roger Clemens, Boston, p		1938	Jimmie Foxx, Boston, 1b
1985	Don Mattingly, New York, 1b		1937	Charlie Gehringer, Detroit, 2b
1984	Willie Hernandez, Detroit, p		1936	Lou Gehrig, New York, 1b
1983	Cal Ripken Jr., Baltimore, ss		1935	*Hank Greenberg, Detroit, 1b
1982	Robin Yount, Milwaukee, ss		1934	Mickey Cochrane, Detroit, c
1981	Rollie Fingers, Milwaukee, p		1933	Jimmie Foxx, Philadelphia, 1b
1980	George Brett, Kansas City, 3b		1932	Jimmie Foxx, Philadelphia, 1b
1979	Don Baylor, California, of		1931	Lefty Grove, Philadelphia, p
1978	Jim Rice, Boston, of			
1977	Rod Carew, Minnesota, 1b			
1976	Thurman Munson, New York, c			

Cy Young Winners (by year)

National League

1975	Fred Lynn, Boston, of		1999	Randy Johnson, Arizona
1974	Jeff Burroughs, Texas, of		1998	Tom Glavine, Atlanta
1973	*Reggie Jackson, Oakland, of		1997	Pedro Martinez, Montreal
1972	Richie Allen, Chicago, 1b		1996	John Smoltz, Atlanta
1971	Vida Blue, Oakland, p		1995	*Greg Maddux, Atlanta
1970	Boog Powell, Baltimore, 1b		1994	*Greg Maddux, Atlanta
1969	Harmon Killebrew, Minn. 1b/3b		1993	Greg Maddux, Atlanta
1968	*Denny McLain, Detroit, p		1992	Greg Maddux, Chicago
1967	Carl Yastrzemski, Boston, of		1991	Tom Glavine, Atlanta
1966	*Frank Robinson, Baltimore, of		1990	Doug Drabek, Pittsburgh
1965	Zoilo Versalles, Minnesota, ss			

1989	Mark Davis, San Diego
1988	*Orel Hershiser, Los Angeles
1987	Steve Bedrosian, Philadelphia
1986	Mike Scott, Houston
1985	Dwight Gooden, New York
1984	*Rick Sutcliffe, Chicago
1983	John Denny, Philadelphia
1982	Steve Carlton, Philadelphia
1981	Fernando Valenzuela, Los Angeles
1980	Steve Carlton, Philadelphia
1979	Bruce Sutter, Chicago
1978	Gaylord Perry, San Diego
1977	*Steve Carlton, Philadelphia
1976	Randy Jones, San Diego
1975	Tom Seaver, New York
1974	Mike Marshall, Los Angeles
1973	Tom Seaver, New York
1972	*Steve Carlton, Philadelphia
1971	Ferguson Jenkins, Chicago
1970	Bob Gibson, St. Louis
1969	Tom Seaver, New York
1968	*Bob Gibson, St. Louis
1967	Mike McCormick, San Francisco
1966	*Sandy Koufax, Los Angeles
1965	*Sandy Koufax, Los Angeles
1963	*Sandy Koufax, Los Angeles
1962	Don Drysdale, Los Angeles
1960	Vernon Law, Pittsburgh
1957	Warren Spahn, Milwaukee
1956	Don Newcombe, Brooklyn

American League

1999	Pedro Martinez, Boston
1998	*Roger Clemens, Toronto
1997	Roger Clemens, Toronto
1996	Pat Hentgen, Toronto
1995	Randy Johnson, Seattle
1994	David Cone, Kansas City
1993	Jack McDowell, Chicago
1992	Dennis Eckersley, Oakland
1991	Roger Clemens, Boston
1990	Bob Welch, Oakland
1989	Bret Saberhagen, Kansas City
1988	Frank Viola, Minnesota
1987	Roger Clemens, Boston
1986	*Roger Clemens, Boston
1985	Bret Saberhagen, Kansas City
1984	Willie Hernandez, Detroit
1983	LaMarr Hoyt, Chicago

1982	Pete Vuckovich, Milwaukee
1981	Rollie Fingers, Milwaukee
1980	Steve Stone, Baltimore
1979	Mike Flanagan, Baltimore
1978	*Ron Guidry, New York
1977	Sparky Lyle, New York
1976	Jim Palmer, Baltimore
1975	Jim Palmer, Baltimore
1974	Catfish Hunter, Oakland
1973	Jim Palmer, Baltimore
1972	Gaylord Perry, Cleveland
1971	Vida Blue, Oakland
1970	Jim Perry, Minnesota
1969	(tie) Mike Cuellar, Baltimore; Denny McLain, Detroit
1968	*Denny McLain, Detroit
1967	Jim Lonborg, Boston
1964	Dean Chance, Los Angeles
1961	Whitey Ford, New York
1959	Early Wynn, Chicago
1958	Bob Turley, New York

Rookie of the Year

National League

1999	Scott Williamson, Cincinnati
1998	Kerry Wood, Chicago
1997	*Scott Rolen, Philadelphia
1996	Todd Hollandsworth, Los Angeles
1995	Hideo Nomo, Los Angeles
1994	*Raul Mondesi, Los Angeles
1993	*Mike Piazza, Los Angeles
1992	Eric Karros, Los Angeles
1991	Jeff Bagwell, Houston
1990	Dave Justice, Atlanta
1989	Jerome Walton, Chicago
1988	Chris Sabo, Cincinnati
1987	*Benito Santiago, San Diego
1986	Todd Worrell, St. Louis
1985	*Vince Coleman, St. Louis
1984	Dwight Gooden, New York
1983	Darryl Strawberry, New York
1982	Steve Sax, Los Angeles
1981	Fernando Valenzuela, Los Angeles
1980	Steve Howe, Los Angeles
1979	Rick Sutcliffe, Los Angeles
1978	Bob Horner, Atlanta
1977	Andre Dawson, Montreal
1976	Butch Metzger, San Diego &

	Pat Zachry, Cincinnati
1975	John Montefusco, San Francisco
1974	Bake McBride, St. Louis
1973	Gary Matthews, San Francisco
1972	Jon Matlack, New York
1971	Earl Williams, Atlanta
1970	Carl Morton, Montreal
1969	Ted Sizemore, Los Angeles
1968	Johnny Bench, Cincinnati
1967	Tom Seaver, New York
1966	Tommy Helms, Cincinnati
1965	Jim Lefebvre, Los Angeles
1964	Richie Allen, Philadelphia
1963	Pete Rose, Cincinnati
1962	Ken Hubbs, Chicago
1961	Billy Williams, Chicago
1960	Frank Howard, Los Angeles
1959	Willie McCovey, San Francisco
1958	Orlando Cepeda, San Francisco
1957	Jack Sanford, Philadelphia
1956	*Frank Robinson, Cincinnati
1955	Bill Virdon, St. Louis
1954	Wally Moon, St. Louis
1953	Jim Gilliam, Brooklyn
1952	Joe Black, Brooklyn
1951	Willie Mays, New York
1950	Sam Jethroe, Boston
1949	Don Newcombe, Brooklyn
1948	Alvin Dark, Boston
1947	Jackie Robinson, Brooklyn

American League

1999	Carlos Beltran, Kansas City
1998	Ben Grieve, Oakland
1997	*Nomar Garciaparra, Boston
1996	*Derek Jeter, New York
1995	Marty Cordova, Minnesota
1994	Bob Hamelin, Kansas City
1993	*Tim Salmon, California
1992	Pat Listach, Milwaukee
1991	Chuck Knoblauch, Minnesota
1990	*Sandy Alomar Jr., Cleveland
1989	Gregg Olson, Baltimore
1988	Walt Weiss, Oakland
1987	*Mark McGwire, Oakland
1986	Jose Canseco, Oakland
1985	Ozzie Guillen, Chicago
1984	Alvin Davis, Seattle
1983	Ron Kittle, Chicago
1982	Cal Ripken Jr., Baltimore

1981	Dave Righetti, New York
1980	Joe Charboneau, Cleveland
1979	John Castino, Minnesota &
	Alfredo Griffin, Toronto
1978	Lou Whitaker, Detroit
1977	Eddie Murray, Baltimore
1976	Mark Fidrych, Detroit
1975	Fred Lynn, Boston
1974	Mike Hargrove, Texas
1973	Al Bumbry, Baltimore
1972	*Carlton Fisk, Boston
1971	Chris Chambliss, Cleveland
1970	Thurman Munson, New York
1969	Lou Pinella, Kansas City
1968	Stan Bahnsen, New York
1967	Rod Carew, Minnesota
1966	Tommie Agee, Chicago
1965	Curt Blefary, Baltimore
1964	Tony Oliva, Minnesota
1963	Gary Peters, Chicago
1962	Tom Tresh, New York
1961	Don Schwall, Boston
1960	Ron Hansen, Baltimore
1959	Bob Allison, Washington
1958	Albie Pearson, Washington
1957	*Tony Kubek, New York
1956	Luis Aparicio, Chicago
1955	Herb Score, Cleveland
1954	Bob Grim, New York
1953	Harvey Kuenn, Detroit
1952	Harry Byrd, Philadelphia
1951	Gil McDougald, New York
1950	Walt Dropo, Boston
1949	Roy Sievers, St. Louis

Batting Average (AVG)
National League

Year		AVG
1999	Larry Walker, Colorado	.379
1998	Larry Walker, Colorado	.363
1997	Tony Gwynn, San Diego	.372
1996	Tony Gwynn, San Diego	.353
1995	Tony Gwynn, San Diego	.368
1994	Tony Gwynn, San Diego	.394
1993	Andres Galarraga, Colorado	.370
1992	Gary Sheffield, San Diego	.330
1991	Terry Pendleton, Atlanta	.319
1990	Willie McGee, St. Louis	.335

Year		AVG
1989	Tony Gwynn, San Diego	.336
1988	Tony Gwynn, San Diego	.313
1987	Tony Gwynn, San Diego	.370
1986	Tim Raines, Montreal	.334
1985	Willie McGee, St. Louis	.353
1984	Tony Gwynn, San Diego	.351
1983	Bill Madlock, Pittsburgh	.323
1982	Al Oliver, Montreal	.331
1981	Bill Madlock, Pittsburgh	.341
1980	Bill Buckner, Chicago	.324
1979	Keith Hernandez, St. Louis	.344
1978	Dave Parker, Pittsburgh	.334
1977	Dave Parker, Pittsburgh	.338
1976	Bill Madlock, Chicago	.339
1975	Bill Madlock, Chicago	.354
1974	Ralph Garr, Atlanta	.353
1973	Pete Rose, Cincinnati	.338
1972	Billy Williams, Chicago	.333
1971	Joe Torre, St. Louis	.363
1970	Rico Carty, Atlanta	.366
1969	Pete Rose, Cincinnati	.348
1968	Pete Rose, Cincinnati	.335
1967	Roberto Clemente, Pittsburgh	.357
1966	Matty Alou, Pittsburgh	.342
1965	Roberto Clemente, Pittsburgh	.329
1964	Roberto Clemente, Pittsburgh	.339
1963	Tommy Davis, Los Angeles	.326
1962	Tommy Davis, Los Angeles	.346
1961	Roberto Clemente, Pittsburgh	.351
1960	Dick Groat, Pittsburgh	.325
1959	Hank Aaron, Milwaukee	.355
1958	Richie Ashburn, Philadelphia	.350
1957	Stan Musial, St. Louis	.351
1956	Hank Aaron, Milwaukee	.328
1955	Richie Ashburn, Philadelphia	.338
1954	Willie Mays, New York	.345
1953	Carl Furillo, Brooklyn	.344
1952	Stan Musial, St. Louis	.336
1951	Stan Musial, St. Louis	.355
1950	Stan Musial, St. Louis	.346
1949	Jackie Robinson, Brooklyn	.342
1948	Stan Musial, St. Louis	.376
1947	Harry Walker, St. Louis-Philadelphia	.363
1946	Stan Musial, St. Louis	.365
1945	Phil Cavarretta, Chicago	.355
1944	Dixie Walker, Brooklyn	.357
1943	Stan Musial, St. Louis	.357
1942	Ernie Lombardi, Boston	.330

Year		AVG
1941	Pete Reiser, Brooklyn	.343
1940	Debs Garms, Pittsburgh	.355
1939	Johnny Mize, St. Louis	.349
1938	Ernie Lombardi, Cincinnati	.342
1937	Joe Medwick, St. Louis	.374
1936	Paul Waner, Pittsburgh	.373
1935	Arky Vaughan, Pittsburgh	.385
1934	Paul Waner, Pittsburgh	.362
1933	Chuck Klein, Philadelphia	.368
1932	Lefty O'Doul, Brooklyn	.368
1931	Chick Hafey, St. Louis	.349
1930	Bill Terry, New York	.401
1929	Lefty O'Doul, Philadelphia	.398
1928	Rogers Hornsby, Boston	.387
1927	Paul Waner, Pittsburgh	.380
1926	Bubbles Hargrave, Cincinnati	.353
1925	Rogers Hornsby, St. Louis	.403
1924	Rogers Hornsby, St. Louis	.424
1923	Rogers Hornsby, St. Louis	.384
1922	Rogers Hornsby, St. Louis	.401
1921	Rogers Hornsby, St. Louis	.397
1920	Rogers Hornsby, St. Louis	.370
1919	Edd Roush, Cincinnati	.321
1918	Zack Wheat, Brooklyn	.335
1917	Edd Roush, Cincinnati	.341
1916	Hal Chase, Cincinnati	.339
1915	Larry Doyle, New York	.320
1914	Jake Daubert, Brooklyn	.329
1913	Jake Daubert, Brooklyn	.350
1912	Heinie Zimmerman, Chicago	.372
1911	Honus Wagner, Pittsburgh	.334
1910	Sherry Magee, Philadelphia	.331
1909	Honus Wagner, Pittsburgh	.339
1908	Honus Wanger, Pittsburgh	.354
1907	Honus Wagner, Pittsburgh	.350
1906	Honus Wagner, Pittsburgh	.339
1905	Cy Semour, Cincinnati	.377
1904	Honus Wagner, Pittsburgh	.349
1903	Honus Wagner, Pittsburgh	.355
1902	Ginger Beaumont, Pittsburgh	.357
1901	Jesse Burkett, St. Louis	.382
1900	Honus Wagner, Pittsburgh	.381

American League

Year		AVG
1999	Nomar Garciaparra, Boston	.357
1998	Bernie Williams, New York	.339
1997	Frank Thomas, Chicago	.347
1996	Alex Rodriguez, Seattle	.358
1995	Edgar Martinez, Seattle	.356

Year		AVG	Year		AVG
1994	Paul O'Neill, New York	.359	1945	Snuffy Stirnweiss, New York	.309
1993	John Olerud, Toronto	.363	1944	Lou Boudreau, Cleveland	.327
1992	Edgar Martinez, Seattle	.343	1943	Luke Appling, Chicago	.328
1991	Julio Franco, Texas	.341	1942	Ted Williams, Boston	.356
1990	George Brett, Kansas City	.329	1941	Ted Williams, Boston	.406
1989	Kirby Puckett, Minnesota	.339	1940	Joe DiMaggio, New York	.352
1988	Wade Boggs, Boston	.366	1939	Joe DiMaggio, New York	.381
1987	Wade Boggs, Boston	.363	1938	Jimmie Foxx, Boston	.349
1986	Wade Boggs, Boston	.357	1937	Charlie Gehringer, Detroit	.371
1985	Wade Boggs, Boston	.368	1936	Luke Appling, Chicago	.388
1984	Don Mattingly, New York	.343	1935	Buddy Myer, Washington	.349
1983	Wade Boggs, Boston	.361	1934	Lou Gehrig, New York	.363
1982	Willie Wilson, Kansas City	.332	1933	Jimmie Foxx, Philadelphia	.356
1981	Carney Lansford, Boston	.336	1932	Dale Alexander, Detroit-Boston	.367
1980	George Brett, Kansas City	.390	1931	Al Simmons, Philadelphia	.390
1979	Fred Lynn, Boston	.333	1930	Al Simmons, Philadelphia	.381
1978	Rod Carew, Minnesota	.333	1929	Lew Fonseca, Cleveland	.369
1977	Rod Carew, Minnesota	.388	1928	Goose Goslin, Washington	.379
1976	George Brett, Kansas City	.333	1927	Harry Heilmann, Detroit	.398
1975	Rod Carew, Minnesota	.359	1926	Heinie Manush, Detroit	.378
1974	Rod Carew, Minnesota	.364	1925	Harry Heilmann, Detroit	.393
1973	Rod Carew, Minnesota	.350	1924	Babe Ruth, New York	.378
1972	Rod Carew, Minnesota	.318	1923	Harry Heilmann, Detroit	.403
1971	Tony Oliva, Minnesota	.337	1922	George Sisler, St. Louis	.420
1970	Alex Johnson, California	.329	1921	Harry Heilmann, Detroit	.394
1969	Rod Carew, Minnesota	.332	1920	George Sisler, St. Louis	.407
1968	Carl Yastrzemski, Boston	.301	1919	Ty Cobb, Detroit	.384
1967	Carl Yastrzemski, Boston	.326	1918	Ty Cobb, Detroit	.382
1966	Frank Robinson, Baltimore	.316	1917	Ty Cobb, Detroit	.383
1965	Tony Oliva, Minnesota	.321	1916	Tris Speaker, Cleveland	.386
1964	Tony Oliva, Minnesota	.323	1915	Ty Cobb, Detroit	.369
1963	Carl Yastrzemski, Boston	.321	1914	Ty Cobb, Detroit	.368
1962	Pete Runnels, Boston	.326	1913	Ty Cobb, Detroit	.390
1961	Norm Cash,* Detroit	.361	1912	Ty Cobb, Detroit	.410
1960	Pete Runnels, Boston	.320	1911	Ty Cobb, Detroit	.420
1959	Harvey Kuenn, Detroit	.353	1910	Ty Cobb, Detroit	.385
1958	Ted Williams, Boston	.328	1909	Ty Cobb, Detroit	.377
1957	Ted Williams, Boston	.388	1908	Ty Cobb, Detroit	.324
1956	Mickey Mantle, New York	.353	1907	Ty Cobb, Detroit	.350
1955	Al Kaline, Detroit	.340	1906	George Stone, St. Louis	.358
1954	Bobby Avila, Cleveland	.341	1905	Elmer Flick, Cleveland	.306
1953	Mickey Vernon, Washington	.337	1904	Nap Lajoie, Cleveland	.381
1952	Ferris Fain, Philadelphia	.327	1903	Nap Lajoie, Cleveland	.355
1951	Ferris Fain, Philadelphia	.344	1902	Ed Delahanty, Washington	.376
1950	Billy Goodman, Boston	.354	1901	Nap Lajoie, Philadelphia	.422
1949	George Kell, Detroit	.343			
1948	Ted Williams, Boston	.369			
1947	Ted Willliams, Boston	.343			
1946	Mickey Vernon, Washington	.353			

*Norm Cash later admitted to using a corked bat the entire season. He played 16 other seasons and never hit better than .286.

Home Runs (HR)

National League

Year		HR
1999	Mark McGwire, St. Louis	65
1998	Mark McGwire, St. Louis	70
1997	Larry Walker, Colorado	49
1996	Andres Galarraga, Colorado	40
1995	Dante Bichette, Colorado	40
1994	Matt Williams, San Francisco	43
1993	Barry Bonds, San Francisco	46
1992	Fred McGriff, San Diego	35
1991	Howard Johnson, New York	38
1990	Ryne Sandberg, Chicago	40
1989	Kevin Mitchell, San Francisco	47
1988	Darryl Strawberry, New York	39
1987	Andre Dawson, Chicago	49
1986	Mike Schmidt, Philadelphia	37
1985	Dale Murphy, Atlanta	37
1984	Dale Murphy, Atlanta	36
	& Mike Schmidt, Philadelphia	36
1983	Mike Schmidt, Philadelphia	40
1982	Dave Kingman, New York	37
1981	Mike Schmidt, Philadelphia	31
1980	Mike Schmidt, Philadelphia	48
1979	Dave Kingman, Chicago	48
1978	George Foster, Cincinnati	40
1977	George Foster, Cincinnati	52
1976	Mike Schmidt, Philadelphia	38
1975	Mike Schmidt, Philadelphia	38
1974	Mike Schmidt, Philadelphia	36
1973	Willie Stargell, Pittsburgh	44
1972	Johnny Bench, Cincinnati	40
1971	Willie Stargell, Pittsburgh	48
1970	Johnny Bench, Cincinnati	45
1969	Willie McCovey, San Francisco	45
1968	Willie McCovey, San Francisco	36
1967	Hank Aaron, Atlanta	39
1966	Hank Aaron, Atlanta	44
1965	Willie Mays, San Francisco	52
1964	Willie Mays, San Francisco	47
1963	Hank Aaron, Milwaukee	44
	& Willie McCovey, San Francisco	44
1962	Willie Mays, San Francisco	49
1961	Orlando Cepeda, San Francisco	46
1960	Ernie Banks, Chicago	41
1959	Eddie Mathews, Milwaukee	46
1958	Ernie Banks, Chicago	47
1957	Hank Aaron, Milwaukee	44

Year		HR
1956	Duke Snider, Brooklyn	43
1955	Willie Mays, New York	51
1954	Ted Kluszewski, Cincinnati	49
1953	Eddie Mathews, Milwaukee	47
1952	Ralph Kiner, Pittsburgh	37
	& Hank Sauer, Chicago	37
1951	Ralph Kiner, Pittsburgh	42
1950	Ralph Kiner, Pittsburgh	47
1949	Ralph Kiner, Pittsburgh	54
1948	Ralph Kiner, Pittsburgh	40
	& Johnny Mize, New York	40
1947	Ralph Kiner, Pittsburgh	51
	& Johnny Mize, New York	51
1946	Ralph Kiner, Pittsburgh	23
1945	Tommy Holmes, Boston	28
1944	Bill Nicholson, Chicago	33
1943	Bill Nicholson, Chicago	29
1942	Mel Ott, New York	30
1941	Dolf Camilli, Brooklyn	34
1940	Johnny Mize, St. Louis	43
1939	Johnny Mize, St. Louis	28
1938	Mel Ott, New York	36
1937	Joe Medwick, St. Louis	31
	& Mel Ott, New York	31
1936	Mel Ott, New York	33
1935	Wally Berger, Boston	34
1934	Rip Collins, St. Louis	35
	& Mel Ott, New York	35
1933	Chuck Klein, Philadelphia	28
1932	Chuck Klein, Philadelphia	38
	& Mel Ott, New York	38
1931	Chuck Klein, Philadelphia	31
1930	Hack Wilson, Chicago	56
1929	Chuck Klein, Philadelphia	43
1928	Jim Bottomley, St. Louis	31
	& Hack Wilson, Chicago	31
1927	Cy Williams, Philadelphia	30
	& Hack Wilson, Chicago	30
1926	Hack Wilson, Chicago	21
1925	Rogers Hornsby, St. Louis	39
1924	Jack Fournier, Brooklyn	27
1923	Cy Williams, Philadelphia	41
1922	Rogers Hornsby, St. Louis	42
1921	George Kelly, New York	23
1920	Cy Williams, Philadelphia	15
1919	Gavvy Cravath, Philadelphia	12
1918	Gavvy Cravath, Philadelphia	8
1917	Gavvy Cravath, Philadelphia	12
	& Dave Robertson, New York	12

Year		HR
1916	Cy Williams, Chicago	12
	& Dave Robertson, New York	12
1915	Gavvy Cravath, Philadelphia	24
1914	Gavvy Cravath, Philadelphia	19
1913	Gavvy Cravath, Philadelphia	19
1912	Heinie Zimmerman, Chicago	14
1911	Wildfire Schulte, Chicago	21
1910	Fred Beck, Boston	10
	&Wildfire Schulte, Chicago	10
1909	Red Murray, New York	7
1908	Tim Jordan, Brooklyn	12
1907	Dave Brain, Boston	10
1906	Tim Jordan, Brooklyn	12
1905	Fred Odwell, Cincinnati	9
1904	Harry Lumley, Brooklyn	9
1903	Jimmy Sheckard, Brooklyn	9
1902	Tommy Leach, Pittsburgh	6
1901	Sam Crawford, Cincinnati	16
1900	Herman Long, Boston	12

Note: In 1997 Mark McGwire hit 58 home runs but hit 34 of them in the American League with Oakland before getting traded to St. Louis.

American League

Year		HR
1999	Ken Griffey Jr., Seattle	48
1998	Ken Griffey Jr., Seattle	56
1997	Ken Griffey Jr., Seattle	56
1996	Mark McGwire, Oakland	52
1995	Albert Belle, Cleveland	50
1994	Ken Griffey Jr., Seattle	40
1993	Juan Gonzalez, Texas	46
1992	Juan Gonzalez, Texas	43
1991	Jose Canseco, Oakland	44
	& Cecil Fielder, Detroit	44
1990	Cecil Fielder, Detroit	51
1989	Fred McGriff, Toronto	36
1988	Jose Canseco, Oakland	42
1987	Mark McGwire, Oakland	49
1986	Jesse Barfield, Toronto	40
1985	Darrell Evans, Detroit	40
1984	Tony Armas, Boston	43
1983	Jim Rice, Boston	39
1982	Reggie Jackson, California	39
	& Gorman Thomas, Milwaukee	39
1981	Tony Armas, Oakland	22
	Dwight Evans, Boston	22
	Bobby Grich, California	22
	& Eddie Murray, Baltimore	22

Year		HR
1980	Reggie Jackson, New York	41
	& Ben Oglivie, Milwaukee	41
1979	Gorman Thomas, Milwaukee	45
1978	Jim Rice, Boston	46
1977	Jim Rice, Boston	39
1976	Graig Nettles, New York	32
1975	Reggie Jackson, Oakland	36
	& George Scott, Milwaukee	36
1974	Dick Allen, Chicago	32
1973	Reggie Jackson, Oakland	32
1972	Dick Allen, Chicago	37
1971	Bill Melton, Chicago	33
1970	Frank Howard, Washington	44
1969	Harmon Killebrew, Minnesota	49
1968	Frank Howard, Washington	44
1967	Harmon Killebrew, Minnesota	44
	& Carl Yastrzemski, Boston	44
1966	Frank Robinson, Baltimore	49
1965	Tony Conigliaro, Boston	32
1964	Harmon Killebrew, Minnesota	49
1963	Harmon Killebrew, Minnesota	45
1962	Harmon Killebrew, Minnesota	48
1961	Roger Maris, New York	61
1960	Mickey Mantle, New York	40
1959	Rocky Colavito, Cleveland	42
	& Harmon Killebrew, Washington	42
1958	Mickey Mantle, New York	42
1957	Roy Sievers, Washington	42
1956	Mickey Mantle, New York	52
1955	Mickey Mantle, New York	37
1954	Larry Doby, Cleveland	32
1953	Al Rosen, Cleveland	43
1952	Larry Doby, Cleveland	32
1951	Gus Zernial, Chicago-Philadelphia	33
1950	Al Rosen, Cleveland	37
1949	Ted Williams, Boston	43
1948	Joe DiMaggio, New York	39
1947	Ted Williams, Boston	32
1946	Hank Greenberg, Detroit	44
1945	Vern Stephens, St. Louis	24
1944	Nick Etten, New York	22
1943	Rudy York, Detroit	34
1942	Ted Williams, Boston	36
1941	Ted Williams, Boston	37
1940	Hank Greenberg, Detroit	41
1939	Jimmie Foxx, Boston	35
1938	Hank Greenberg, Detroit	58
1937	Joe DiMaggio, New York	46
1936	Lou Gehrig, New York	49

Year		HR		Year		RBI
1935	Jimmie Foxx, Philadelphia	36		1998	Sammy Sosa, Chicago	158
	& Hank Greenberg, Detroit	36		1997	Andres Galarraga, Colorado	140
1934	Lou Gehrig, New York	49		1996	Andres Galarraga, Colorado	150
1933	Jimmie Foxx, Philadelphia	48		1995	Dante Bichette, Colorado	128
1932	Jimmie Foxx, Philadelphia	58		1994	Jeff Bagwell, Houston	116
1931	Lou Gehrig, New York	46		1993	Barry Bonds, San Francisco	123
	& Babe Ruth, New York	46		1992	Darren Daulton, Philadelphia	109
1930	Babe Ruth, New York	49		1991	Howard Johnson, New York	117
1929	Babe Ruth, New York	46		1990	Matt Williams, San Francisco	122
1928	Babe Ruth, New York	54		1989	Kevin Mitchell, San Francisco	125
1927	Babe Ruth, New York	60		1988	Will Clark, San Francisco	109
1926	Babe Ruth, New York	47		1987	Andre Dawson, Chicago	137
1925	Bob Meusel, New York	33		1986	Mike Schmidt, Philadelphia	119
1924	Babe Ruth, New York	46		1985	Dave Parker, Cincinnati	125
1923	Babe Ruth, New York	41		1984	Gary Carter, Montreal	106
1922	Ken Williams, St. Louis	39		1984	& Mike Schmidt, Philadelphia	106
1921	Babe Ruth, New York	59		1983	Dale Murphy, Atlanta	121
1920	Babe Ruth, New York	54		1982	Dale Murphy, Atlanta	109
1919	Babe Ruth, Boston	29		1982	& Al Oliver, Montreal	109
1918	Babe Ruth, Boston	11		1981	Mike Schmidt, Philadelphia	91
	& Tilly Walker, Philadelphia	11		1980	Mike Schmidt, Philadelphia	121
1917	Wally Pipp, New York	9		1979	Dave Winfield, San Diego	118
1916	Wally Pipp, New York	12		1978	George Foster, Cincinnati	120
1915	Braggo Roth, Chicago-Cleveland	7		1977	George Foster, Cincinnati	149
1914	Home Run Baker, Philadelphia	9		1976	George Foster, Cincinnati	121
1913	Home Run Baker, Philadelphia	12		1975	Greg Luzinski, Philadelphia	120
1912	Home Run Baker, Philadelphia	10		1974	Johnny Bench, Cincinnati	129
	& Tris Speaker, Boston	10		1973	Willie Stargell, Pittsburgh	119
1911	Home Run Baker, Philadelphia	11		1972	Johnny Bench, Cincinnati	125
1910	Jake Stahl, Boston	10		1971	Joe Torre, St. Louis	137
1909	Ty Cobb, Detroit	9		1970	Johnny Bench, Cincinnati	148
1908	Sam Crawford, Detroit	7		1969	Willie McCovey, San Francisco	126
1907	Harry Davis, Philadelphia	8		1968	Willie McCovey, San Francisco	105
1906	Harry Davis, Philadelphia	12		1967	Orlando Cepeda, St. Louis	111
1905	Harry Davis, Philadelphia	8		1966	Hank Aaron, Atlanta	127
1904	Harry Davis, Philadelphia	10		1965	Deron Johnson, Cincinnati	130
1903	Buck Freeman, Boston	13		1964	Ken Boyer, St. Louis	119
1902	Socks Seybold, Philadelphia	16		1963	Hank Aaron, Milwaukee	130
1901	Nap Lajoie, Philadelphia	14		1962	Tommy Davis, Los Angeles	153
				1961	Orlando Cepeda, San Francisco	142
				1960	Hank Aaron, Milwaukee	126
				1959	Ernie Banks, Chicago	143
				1958	Ernie Banks, Chicago	129
				1957	Hank Aaron, Milwaukee	132
				1956	Stan Musial, St. Louis	109
				1955	Duke Snider, Brooklyn	136
				1954	Ted Kluszewski, Cincinnati	141
				1953	Roy Campanella, Brooklyn	142
				1952	Hank Sauer, Chicago	121

Note: In 1997 Mark McGwire hit 58 home runs but hit 24 of them in the National League with St. Louis after getting traded from Oakland.

Runs Batted In (RBI)

National League

Year		RBI
1999	Mark McGwire, St. Louis	147

Year		RBI
1951	Monte Irvin, New York	121
1950	Del Ennis, Philadelphia	126
1949	Ralph Kiner, Pittsburgh	127
1948	Stan Musial, St. Louis	131
1947	Johnny Mize, New York	138
1946	Enos Slaughter, St. Louis	130
1945	Dixie Walker, Brooklyn	124
1944	Bill Nicholson, Chicago	122
1943	Bill Nicholson, Chicago	128
1942	Johnny Mize, New York	110
1941	Dolph Camilli, Brooklyn	120
1940	Johnny Mize, St. Louis	137
1939	Frank McCormick, Cincinnati	128
1938	Joe Medwick, St. Louis	122
1937	Joe Medwick, St. Louis	154
1936	Joe Medwick, St. Louis	138
1935	Wally Berger, Boston	130
1934	Mel Ott, New York	135
1933	Chuck Klein, Philadelphia	120
1932	Don Hurst, Philadelphia	143
1931	Chuck Klein, Philadelphia	121
1930	Hack Wilson, Chicago	190
1929	Hack Wilson, Chicago	159
1928	Jim Bottomley, St. Louis	136
1927	Paul Waner, Pittsburgh	131
1926	Jim Bottomley, St. Louis	120
1925	Rogers Hornsby, St. Louis	143
1924	George Kelly, New York	136
1923	Irish Meusel, New York	125
1922	Rogers Hornsby, St. Louis	152
1921	Rogers Hornsby, St. Louis	126
1920	Rogers Hornsby, St. Louis	94
	& George Kelly, New York	94
1919	Hy Myers, Brooklyn	73
1918	Sherry Magee, Cincinnati	76
1917	Heinie Zimmerman, New York	102
1916	Heinie Zimmerman,	
	Chicago-New York	83
1915	Gavvy Cravath, Philadelphia	115
1914	Sherry Magee, Philadelphia	103
1913	Gavvy Cravath, Philadelphia	128
1912	Heinie Zimmerman, Chicago	103
1911	Wildfire Schulte, Chicago	121
1910	Sherry Magee, Philadelphia	123
1909	Honus Wagner, Pittsburgh	100
1908	Honus Wagner, Pittsburgh	109
1907	Sherry Magee, Philadelphia	85
1906	Jim Nealon, Pittsburgh	83
	& Harry Steinfeldt, Chicago	83

Year		RBI
1905	Cy Seymour, Cincinnati	121
1904	Bill Dahlen, New York	80
1903	Sam Mertes, New York	104
1902	Honus Wagner, Pittsburgh	91
1901	Honus Wagner, Pittsburgh	126
1900	Elmer Flick, Philadelphia	110

American League

Year		RBI
1999	Manny Ramirez, Cleveland	165
1998	Juan Gonzalez, Texas	157
1997	Ken Griffey Jr., Seattle	147
1996	Albert Belle, Cleveland	148
1995	Albert Belle, Cleveland	126
	& Mo Vaughn, Boston	126
1994	Kirby Puckett, Minnesota	112
1993	Albert Belle, Cleveland	129
1992	Cecil Fielder, Detroit	124
1991	Cecil Fielder, Detroit	133
1990	Cecil Fielder, Detroit	132
1989	Ruben Sierra, Texas	119
1988	Jose Canseco, Oakland	124
1987	George Bell, Toronto	134
1986	Joe Carter, Cleveland	121
1985	Don Mattingly, New York	145
1984	Tony Armas, Boston	123
1983	Cecil Cooper, Milwaukee	126
	& Jim Rice, Boston	126
1982	Hal McRae, Kansas City	133
1981	Eddie Murray, Baltimore	78
1980	Cecil Cooper, Milwaukee	122
1979	Don Baylor, California	139
1978	Jim Rice, Boston	139
1977	Larry Hisle, Minnesota	119
1976	Lee May, Baltimore	109
1975	George Scott, Milwaukee	109
1974	Jeff Burroughs, Texas	118
1973	Reggie Jackson, Oakland	117
1972	Dick Allen, Chicago	113
1971	Harmon Killebrew, Minnesota	119
1970	Frank Howard, Washington	126
1969	Harmon Killebrew, Minnesota	140
1968	Ken Harrelson, Boston	109
1967	Carl Yastrzemski, Boston	121
1966	Frank Robinson, Baltimore	122
1965	Rocky Colavito, Cleveland	108
1964	Brooks Robinson, Baltimore	118
1963	Dick Stuart, Boston	118
1962	Harmon Killebrew, Minnesota	126

Year		RBI
1961	Roger Maris, New York	142
1960	Roger Maris, New York	112
1959	Jackie Jensen, Boston	112
1958	Jackie Jensen, Boston	122
1957	Roy Sievers, Washington	114
1956	Mickey Mantle, New York	130
1955	Ray Boone, Detroit	116
	& Jackie Jensen, Boston	116
1954	Larry Doby, Cleveland	126
1953	Al Rosen, Cleveland	145
1952	Al Rosen, Cleveland	105
1951	Gus Zernial, Chicago-Philadelphia	129
1950	Walt Dropo, Boston	144
	&Vern Stephens, Boston	144
1949	Ted Williams, Boston	159
	&Vern Stephens, Boston	159
1948	Joe DiMaggio, New York	155
1947	Ted Williams, Boston	114
1946	Hank Greenberg, Detroit	127
1945	Nick Etten, New York	111
1944	Vern Stephens, St. Louis	109
1943	Rudy York, Detroit	118
1942	Ted Williams, Boston	137
1941	Joe DiMaggio, New York	125
1940	Hank Greenberg, Detroit	150
1939	Ted Williams, Boston	145
1938	Jimmie Foxx, Boston	175
1937	Hank Greenberg, Detroit	183
1936	Hal Trosky, Cleveland	162
1935	Hank Greenberg, Detroit	170
1934	Lou Gehrig, New York	165
1933	Jimmie Foxx, Philadelphia	163
1932	Jimmie Foxx, Philadelphia	169
1931	Lou Gehrig, New York	184
1930	Lou Gehrig, New York	174
1929	Al Simmons, Philadelphia	157
1928	Lou Gehrig, New York	142
	& Babe Ruth, New York	142
1927	Lou Gehrig, New York	175
1926	Babe Ruth, New York	145
1925	Bob Meusel, New York	138
1924	Goose Goslin, Washington	129
1923	Babe Ruth, New York	131
1922	Ken Williams, St. Louis	155
1921	Babe Ruth, New York	171
1920	Babe Ruth, New York	137
1919	Babe Ruth, Boston	114
1918	Bobby Veach, Detroit	78

Year		RBI
1917	Bobby Veach, Detroit	103
1916	Del Pratt, St. Louis	103
1915	Sam Crawford, Detroit	112
	& Bobby Veach, Detroit	112
1914	Sam Crawford, Detroit	104
1913	Home Run Baker, Philadelphia	126
1912	Home Run Baker, Philadelphia	133
1911	Ty Cobb, Detroit	144
1910	Sam Crawford, Detroit	120
1909	Ty Cobb, Detroit	107
1908	Ty Cobb, Detroit	108
1907	Ty Cobb, Detroit	116
1906	Harry Davis, Philadelphia	96
1905	Harry Davis, Philadelphia	83
1904	Nap Lajoie, Cleveland	102
1903	Buck Freeman, Boston	104
1902	Buck Freeman, Boston	121
1901	Nap Lajoie, Philadelphia	125

Annual Pitching Leaders

Note: Winning Percentage (Pct)
At least 15 wins, except in strike years of 1981 and 1994 (when the minimum was 10).

National League

Year		Won-Lost	Pct
1999	Mike Hampton, Houston	22-4	.846
1998	John Smoltz, Atlanta	17-3	.850
1997	Greg Maddux, Atlanta	19-4	.826
1996	John Smoltz, Atlanta	24-8	.750
1995	Greg Maddux, Atlanta	19-2	.905
1994	Marvin Freeman, Colorado	10-2	.833
1993	Mark Portugal, Houston	18-4	.818
1992	Bob Tewksbury, St. Louis	16-5	.762
1991	John Smiley, Pittsburgh	20-8	.714
	& Jose Rijo, Cincinnati	15-6	.714
1990	Doug Drabek, Pittsburgh	22-6	.786
1989	Mike Bielecki, Chicago	18-7	.720
1988	David Cone, New York	20-3	.870
1987	Dwight Gooden, New York	15-7	.682
1986	Bob Ojeda, New York	18-5	.783
1985	Orel Hershiser, Los Angeles	19-3	.864
1984	Rick Sutcliffe, Chicago	16-1	.941
1983	John Denny, Philadelphia	19-6	.760
1982	Phil Niekro, Atlanta	17-4	.810
1981	Tom Seaver, Cincinnati	14-2	.875
1980	Jim Bibby, Pittsburgh	19-6	.760

Year		Won-Lost	Pct
1979	Tom Seaver, Cincinnati	16-6	.727
1978	Gaylord Perry, San Diego	21-6	.778
1977	John Candelaria, Pittsburgh	20-5	.800
1976	Steve Carlton, Philadelphia	20-7	.741
1975	Don Gullett, Cincinnati	15-4	.789
1974	Andy Messersmith,		
	Los Angeles	20-6	.769
1973	Tommy John, Los Angeles	16-7	.696
1972	Gary Nolan, Cincinnati	15-5	.750
1971	Don Gullett, Cincinnati	16-6	.727
1970	Bob Gibson, St. Louis	23-7	.767
1969	Tom Seaver, New York	25-7	.781
1968	Steve Blass, Pittsburgh	18-6	.750
1967	Dick Hughes, St. Louis	16-6	.727
1966	Juan Marichal,		
	San Francisco	25-6	.806
1965	Sandy Koufax, Los Angeles	26-8	.765
1964	Sandy Koufax, Los Angeles	19-5	.792
1963	Ron Perranoski,		
	Los Angeles	16-3	.842
1962	Bob Purkey, Cincinnati	23-5	.821
1961	Johnny Podres,		
	Los Angeles	18-5	.783
1960	Ernie Broglio, St. Louis	21-9	.700
1959	Roy Face, Pittsburgh	18-1	.947
1958	Warren Spahn, Milwaukee	22-11	.667
	& Lew Burdette,		
	Milwaukee	20-10	.667
1957	Bob Buhl, Milwaukee	18-7	.720
1956	Don Newcombe, Brooklyn	27-7	.794
1955	Don Newcombe, Brooklyn	20-5	.800
1954	Johnny Antonelli,		
	New York	21-7	.750
1953	Carl Erskine, Brooklyn	20-6	.769
1952	Hoyt Wilhelm, New York	15-3	.833
1951	Preacher Roe, Brooklyn	22-3	.880
1950	Sal Maglie, New York	18-4	.818
1949	Preacher Roe, Brooklyn	15-6	.714
1948	Harry Brecheen, St. Louis	20-7	.741
1947	Larry Jansen, New York	21-5	.808
1946	Murray Dickson, St. Louis	15-6	.714
1945	Harry Brecheen, St. Louis	14-4	.778
1944	Ted Wilks, St. Louis	17-4	.810
1943	Mort Cooper, St. Louis	21-8	.724
1942	Larry French, Brooklyn	15-4	.789
1941	Elmer Riddle, Cincinnati	19-4	.826
1940	Freddie Fitzsimmons,		
	Brooklyn	16-2	.889
1939	Paul Derringer, Cincinnati	25-7	.781

Year		Won-Lost	Pct
1938	Bill Lee, Chicago	22-9	.710
1937	Carl Hubbell, New York	22-8	.733
1936	Carl Hubbell, New York	26-6	.813
1935	Bill Lee, Chicago	20-6	.769
1934	Dizzy Dean, St. Louis	30-7	.811
1933	Ben Cantwell, Boston	20-10	.667
1932	Lon Warneke, Chicago	22-6	.786
1931	Paul Derringer, St. Louis	18-8	.692
1930	Freddie Fitzsimmons,		
	New York	19-7	.731
1929	Charlie Root, Chicago	19-6	.760
1928	Larry Benton, New York	25-9	.735
1927	Larry Benton,		
	Boston-New York	17-7	.708
1926	Ray Kremer, Pittsburgh	20-6	.769
1925	Bill Sherdel, St. Louis	15-6	.714
1924	Emil Yde, Pittsburgh	16-3	.842
1923	Dolf Luque, Cincinnati	27-8	.771
1922	Pete Donohue, Cincinnati	18-9	.677
1921	Bill Doak, St. Louis	15-6	.714
1920	Burleigh Grimes,		
	Brooklyn	23-11	.676
1919	Dutch Reuther, Cincinnati	19-6	.760
1918	Claude Hendrix, Chicago	19-7	.731
1917	Ferdie Schupp, New York	21-7	.750
1916	Tom Hughes, Boston	16-3	.842
1915	Grover Alexander,		
	Philadelphia	31-10	.756
1914	Bill James, Boston	26-7	.788
1913	Bert Humphries, Chicago	16-4	.800
1912	Claude Hendrix, Pittsburgh	24-9	.727
1911	Rube Marquard, New York	24-7	.774
1910	King Cole, Chicago	20-4	.833
1909	Howie Camnitz, Pittsburgh	25-6	.806
	& Christy Mathewson,		
	New York	25-6	.806
1908	Ed Reulbach, Chicago	24-7	.774
1907	Ed Reulbach, Chicago	17-4	.810
1906	Ed Reulbach, Chicago	19-4	.826
1905	Christy Mathewson,		
	New York	31-8	.795
1904	Joe McGinnity, New York	35-8	.814
1903	Sam Leever, Pittsburgh	25-7	.781
1902	Jack Chesbro, Pittsburgh	28-6	.824
1901	Jack Chesbro, Pittsburgh	21-10	.677
1900	Jesse Tannehill, Pittsburgh	20-6	.769

Note: In 1984, Sutcliffe was also 4-5 with Cleveland for a combined AL-NL record of 20-6 (.769).

American League

Year		Won-Lost	Pct
1999	Pedro Martinez, Boston	23-4	.852
1998	David Wells, New York	18-4	.818
1997	Randy Johnson, Seattle	20-4	.833
1996	Charles Nagy, Cleveland	17-5	.773
1995	Randy Johnson, Seattle	18-2	.900
1994	Jason Bere, Chicago	12-2	.857
1993	Jimmy Key, New York	18-6	.750
1992	Mike Mussina, Baltimore	18-5	.783
1991	Scott Erickson, Minnesota	20-8	.714
1990	Bob Welch, Oakland	27-6	.818
1989	Bret Saberhagen, Kansas City	23-6	.793
1988	Frank Viola, Minnesota	24-7	.774
1987	Roger Clemens, Boston	20-9	.690
1986	Roger Clemens, Boston	24-4	.857
1985	Ron Guidry, New York	22-6	.786
1984	Doyle Alexander, Toronto	17-6	.739
1983	Rich Dotson, Chicago	22-7	.759
1982	Pete Vuckovich, Milwaukee	18-6	.750
1981	Pete Vuckovich, Milwaukee	14-4	.778
1980	Steve Stone, Baltimore	25-7	.781
1979	Mike Caldwell, Milwaukee	16-6	.727
1978	Ron Guidry, New York	25-3	.893
1977	Paul Splittorff, Kansas City	16-6	.727
1976	Bill Campbell, Minnesota	17-5	.773
1975	Mike Torrez, Baltimore	20-9	.690
1974	Mike Cuellar, Baltimore	22-10	.688
1973	Catfish Hunter, Oakland	21-5	.808
1972	Catfish Hunter, Oakland	21-7	.750
1971	Dave McNally, Baltimore	21-5	.808
1970	Mike Cuellar, Baltimore	24-8	.750
1969	Jim Palmer, Baltimore	16-4	.800
1968	Denny McLain, Detroit	31-6	.838
1967	Joe Horlen, Chicago	19-7	.731
1966	Sonny Siebert, Cleveland	16-8	.667
1965	Mudcat Grant, Minnesota	21-7	.750
1964	Wally Bunker, Baltimore	19-5	.792
1963	Whitey Ford, New York	24-7	.774
1962	Ray Herbert, Chicago	20-9	.690
	& Jim Palmer, Baltimore	15-5	.750
1961	Whitey Ford, New York	25-4	.862
1960	Jim Perry, Cleveland	18-10	.643
1959	Bob Shaw, Chicago	18-6	.750
1958	Bob Turley, New York	21-7	.750
1957	Dick Donovan, Chicago	16-6	.727
	& Tom Sturdivant, New York	16-6	.727
1956	Whitey Ford, New York	19-6	.760
1955	Tommy Byrne, New York	16-5	.762

Year		Won-Lost	Pct
1954	Sandy Consuegra, Chicago	16-3	.842
1953	Ed Lopat, New York	16-4	.800
1952	Bobby Shantz, Philadelphia	24-7	.774
1951	Bob Feller, Cleveland	22-8	.733
1950	Vic Raschi, New York	21-8	.724
1949	Ellis Kinder, Boston	23-6	.793
1948	Jack Kramer, Boston	18-5	.783
1947	Allie Reynolds, New York	19-8	.704
1946	Boo Ferriss, Boston	25-6	.806
1945	Hal Newhouser, Detroit	25-9	.735
1944	Texas Hughson, Boston	18-5	.783
1943	Spud Chandler, New York	20-4	.833
1942	Ernie Bonham, New York	21-5	.808
1941	Lefty Gomez, New York	15-5	.750
1940	Schoolboy Rowe, Detroit	16-3	.842
1939	Lefty Grove, Boston	15-4	.789
1938	Red Ruffing, New York	21-7	.750
1937	Johnny Allen, Cleveland	15-1	.938
1936	Monte Pearson, New York	19-7	.731
1935	Eldon Auker, Detroit	18-7	.720
1934	Lefty Gomez, New York	26-5	.839
1933	Lefty Grove, Philadelphia	24-8	.750
1932	Johnny Allen, New York	17-4	.810
1931	Lefty Grove, Philadelphia	31-4	.886
1930	Lefty Grove, Philadelphia	28-5	.848
1929	Lefty Grove, Philadelphia	20-6	.769
1928	General Crowder, St. Louis	21-5	.808
1927	Waite Hoyt, New York	22-7	.759
1926	George Uhle, Cleveland	27-11	.711
1925	Stan Coveleski, Washington	20-5	.800
1924	Walter Johnson, Washington	23-7	.767
1923	Herb Pennock, New York	19-6	.760
1922	Joe Bush, New York	26-7	.788
1921	Carl Mays, New York	27-9	.750
1920	Jim Bagby, Cleveland	31-12	.721
1919	Eddie Cicotte, Chicago	29-7	.806
1918	Sad Sam Jones, Boston	16-5	.762
1917	Reb Russell, Chicago	15-5	.750
1916	Eddie Cicotte, Chicago	15-7	.682
1915	Smokey Joe Wood, Boston	15-5	.750
1914	Chief Bender, Philadelphia	17-3	.850
1913	Walter Johnson, Washington	36-7	.837
1912	Smokey Joe Wood, Boston	34-5	.872
1911	Chief Bender, Philadelphia	17-5	.773
1910	Chief Bender, Philadelphia	23-5	.821
1909	George Mullin, Detroit	29-8	.784
1908	Ed Walsh, Chicago	40-15	.727
1907	Wild Bill Donovan, Detroit	25-4	.862
1906	Eddie Plank, Philadelphia	19-6	.760

Year		Won-Lost	Pct
1905	Andy Coakley, Philadelphia	20-7	.741
1904	Jack Chesbro, New York	41-12	.774
1903	Cy Young, Boston	28-9	.757
1902	Bill Bernhard,		
	Philadelphia-Cleveland	18-5	.783
1901	Clark Griffith, Chicago	24-7	.774

Earned Run Average (ERA)

Earned Run Averages were based on at least 10 complete games pitched (1900–49), at least 154 innings pitched (1950–60), and at least 162 innings pitched since 1961 in the AL and 1962 in the NL. In the strike years of 1981, 1994 and 1995, qualifiers had to pitch at least as many innings as the total number of games their team played that season.

National League

Year		ERA
1999	Randy Johnson, Arizona	2.48
1998	Greg Maddux, Atlanta	2.22
1997	Pedro Martinez, Montreal	1.90
1996	Kevin Brown, Florida	1.89
1995	Greg Maddux, Atlanta	1.63
1994	Greg Maddux, Atlanta	1.56
1993	Greg Maddux, Atlanta	2.36
1992	Bill Swift, San Francisco	2.08
1991	Dennis Martinez, Montreal	2.39
1990	Danny Darwin, Houston	2.21
1989	Scott Garrelts, San Francisco	2.28
1988	Joe Magrane, St. Louis	2.18
1987	Nolan Ryan, Houston	2.76
1986	Mike Scott, Houston	2.22
1985	Dwight Gooden, New York	1.53
1984	Alejandro Peña, Los Angeles	2.48
1983	Atlee Hammaker, San Francisco	2.25
1982	Stever Rogers, Montreal	2.40
1981	Nolan Ryan, Houston	1.69
1980	Don Sutton, Los Angeles	2.21
1979	J.R. Richard, Houston	2.71
1978	Craig Swan, New York	2.43
1977	John Candelaria, Pittsburgh	2.34
1976	John Denny, St. Louis	2.52
1975	Randy Jones, San Diego	2.24
1974	Buzz Capra, Atlanta	2.28
1973	Tom Seaver, New York	2.08
1972	Steve Carlton, Philadelphia	1.97
1971	Tom Seaver, New York	1.76

Year		ERA
1970	Tom Seaver, New York	2.81
1969	Juan Marichal, San Francisco	2.10
1968	Bob Gibson, St. Louis	1.12
1967	Phil Niekro, Atlanta	1.87
1966	Sandy Koufax, Los Angeles	1.73
1965	Sandy Koufax, Los Angeles	2.04
1964	Sandy Koufax, Los Angeles	1.74
1963	Sandy Koufax, Los Angeles	1.88
1962	Sandy Koufax, Los Angeles	2.54
1961	Warren Spahn, Milwaukee	3.02
1960	Mike McCormick, San Francisco	2.70
1959	Sam Jones, San Francisco	2.83
1958	Stu Miller, San Francisco	2.47
1957	Johnny Podres, Brooklyn	2.66
1956	Lew Burdette, Milwaukee	2.70
1955	Bob Friend, Pittsburgh	2.83
1954	Johnny Antonelli, New York	2.30
1953	Warren Spahn, Milwaukee	2.10
1952	Hoyt Wilhelm, New York	2.43
1951	Chet Nichols, Boston	2.88
1950	Jim Hearn, St. Louis-New York	2.50
1949	Dave Koslo, New York	2.50
1948	Harry Brecheen, St. Louis	2.24
1947	Warren Spahn, Boston	2.33
1946	Howie Pollet, St. Louis	2.10
1945	Hank Borowy, Chicago	2.13
1944	Ed Heusser, Cincinnati	2.38
1943	Howie Pollet, St. Louis	1.75
1942	Mort Cooper, St. Louis	1.78
1941	Elmer Riddle, Cincinnati	2.24
1940	Bucky Walters, Cincinnati	2.48
1939	Bucky Walters, Cincinnati	2.29
1938	Bill Lee, Chicago	2.66
1937	Jim Turner, Boston	2.38
1936	Carl Hubbell, New York	2.31
1935	Cy Blanton, Pittsburgh	2.58
1934	Carl Hubbell, New York	2.30
1933	Carl Hubbell, New York	1.66
1932	Lon Warneke, Chicago	2.37
1931	Bill Walker, New York	2.26
1930	Dazzy Vance, Brooklyn	2.61
1929	Bill Walker, New York	3.09
1928	Dazzy Vance, Brooklyn	2.09
1927	Ray Kremer, Pittsburgh	2.47
1926	Ray Kremer, Pittsburgh	2.61
1925	Dolf Luque, Cincinnati	2.63
1924	Dazzy Vance, Brooklyn	2.16
1923	Dolf Luque, Cincinnati	1.93
1922	Rosy Ryan, New York	3.01

Year		ERA
1921	Bill Doak, St. Louis	2.59
1920	Grover Alexander, Chicago	1.91
1919	Grover Alexander, Chicago	1.72
1918	Hippo Vaughn, Chicago	1.74
1917	Grover Alexander, Philadelphia	1.86
1916	Grover Alexander, Philadelphia	1.55
1915	Grover Alexander, Philadelphia	1.22
1914	Bill Doak, St. Louis	1.72
1913	Christy Mathewson, New York	2.06
1912	Jeff Tesreau, New York	1.96
1911	Christy Mathewson, New York	1.99
1910	George McQuillan, Philadelphia	1.60
1909	Christy Mathewson, New York	1.14
1908	Christy Mathewson, New York	1.43
1907	Jack Pfiester, Chicago	1.15
1906	Three Finger Brown, Chicago	1.04
1905	Christy Mathewson, New York	1.27
1904	Joe McGinnity, New York	1.61
1903	Sam Leever, Pittsburgh	2.06
1902	Jack Taylor, Chicago	1.33
1901	Jesse Tannehill, Pittsburgh	2.18
1900	Rube Waddell, Pittsburgh	2.37

Note: In 1945, Borowy had a 3.13 ERA in 18 games with New York (AL) for a combined ERA of 2.65.

American League

1999	Pedro Martinez, Boston	2.07
1998	Roger Clemens, Toronto	2.65
1997	Roger Clemens, Toronto	2.05
1996	Juan Guzman, Toronto	2.93
1995	Randy Johnson, Seattle	2.48
1994	Steve Ontiveros, Oakland	2.65
1993	Kevin Appier, Kansas City	2.56
1992	Roger Clemens, Boston	2.41
1991	Roger Clemens, Boston	2.62
1990	Roger Clemens, Boston	1.93
1989	Bret Saberhagen, Kansas City	2.16
1988	Allan Anderson, Minnesota	2.45
1987	Jimmy Key, Toronto	2.76
1986	Roger Clemens, Boston	2.48
1985	Dave Stieb, Toronto	2.48
1984	Mike Boddicker, Baltimore	2.79
1983	Rick Honeycutt, Texas	2.42
1982	Rick Sutcliffe, Cleveland	2.96
1981	Steve McCatty, Oakland	2.32
1980	Rudy May, New York	2.47
1979	Ron Guidry, New York	2.78

Year		ERA
1978	Ron Guidry, New York	1.74
1977	Frank Tanana, California	2.54
1976	Mark Fidrych, Detroit	2.34
1975	Jim Palmer, Baltimore	2.09
1974	Catfish Hunter, Oakland	2.49
1973	Jim Palmer, Baltimore	2.40
1972	Luis Tiant, Boston	1.91
1971	Vida Blue, Oakland	1.82
1970	Diego Segui, Oakland	2.56
1969	Dick Bosman, Washington	2.19
1968	Luis Tiant, Cleveland	1.60
1967	Joe Horlen, Chicago	2.06
1966	Gary Peters, Chicago	1.98
1965	Sam McDowell, Cleveland	2.18
1964	Dean Chance, Los Angeles	1.65
1963	Gary Peters, Chicago	2.33
1962	Hank Aguirre, Detroit	2.21
1961	Dick Donovan, Washington	2.40
1960	Frank Baumann, Chicago	2.67
1959	Hoyt Wilhelm, Baltimore	2.19
1958	Whitey Ford, New York	2.01
1957	Bobby Shantz, New York	2.45
1956	Whitey Ford, New York	2.47
1955	Billy Pierce, Chicago	1.97
1954	Mike Garcia, Cleveland	2.64
1953	Ed Lopat, New York	2.42
1952	Allie Reynolds, New York	2.06
1951	Saul Rogovin, Detroit-Chicago	2.78
1950	Early Wynn, Cleveland	3.20
1949	Mel Parnell, Boston	2.77
1948	Gene Bearden, Cleveland	2.43
1947	Spud Chandler, New York	2.46
1946	Hal Newhouser, Detroit	1.94
1945	Hal Newhouser, Detroit	1.81
1944	Dizzy Trout, Detroit	2.12
1943	Spud Chandler, New York	1.64
1942	Ted Lyons, Chicago	2.10
1941	Thornton Lee, Chicago	2.37
1940	Ernie Bonham, New York	1.90
1939	Lefty Grove, Boston	2.54
1938	Lefty Grove, Boston	3.08
1937	Lefty Gomez, New York	2.33
1936	Lefty Grove, Boston	2.81
1935	Lefty Grove, Boston	2.70
1934	Lefty Gomez, New York	2.33
1933	Monte Pearson, Cleveland	2.33
1932	Lefty Grove, Philadelphia	2.84
1931	Lefty Grove, Philadelphia	2.06
1930	Lefty Grove, Philadelphia	2.54

Year		ERA	Year		ERA
1929	Lefty Grove, Philadelphia	2.81	1914	Dutch Leonard, Boston	1.01
1928	Garland Braxton, Washington	2.51	1913	Walter Johnson, Washington	1.09
1927	Wilcy Moore, New York	2.28	1912	Walter Johnson, Washington	1.39
1926	Lefty Grove, Philadelphia	2.51	1911	Vean Gregg, Cleveland	1.81
1925	Stan Coveleski, Washington	2.84	1910	Ed Walsh, Chicago	1.27
1924	Walter Johnson, Washington	2.72	1909	Harry Krause, Philadelphia	1.39
1923	Stan Coveleski, Cleveland	2.76	1908	Addie Joss, Cleveland	1.16
1922	Red Faber, Chicago	2.80	1907	Ed Walsh, Chicago	1.60
1921	Red Faber, Chicago	2.48	1906	Doc White, Chicago	1.52
1920	Bob Shawkey, New York	2.45	1905	Rube Waddell, Philadelphia	1.48
1919	Walter Johnson, Washington	1.49	1904	Addie Joss, Cleveland	1.59
1918	Walter Johnson, Washington	1.27	1903	Earl Moore, Cleveland	1.77
1917	Eddie Cicotte, Chicago	1.53	1902	Ed Siever, Detroit	1.91
1916	Babe Ruth, Boston	1.75	1901	Cy Young, Boston	1.62
1915	Smokey Joe Wood, Boston	1.49			

Notes

Introduction

1. Quoted in Justin Kaplan, ed., *Bartlett's Familiar Quotations,* 16th ed. Boston: Little, Brown, 1992, p. 721.
2. Quoted in Bob Chieger, ed., *Voices of Baseball.* New York: New American Library, 1983, p. 4.
3. Roger Angell, *The Summer Game.* New York: Popular Library, 1972, p. 320.
4. Jim Bouton, *Ball Four.* New York: Dell, 1971, p. 369.

Chapter 1: From Across the Ocean

5. Quoted in Mark Alvarez, *The Old Ball Game.* Alexandria, VA: Redefinition, 1990, p. 34.
6. Quoted in Alvarez, *The Old Ball Game,* p. 47.
7. Quoted in Alvarez, *The Old Ball Game,* p. 64.
8. Quoted in Geoffrey C. Ward and Ken Burns, *Baseball: An Illustrated History.* New York: Alfred A. Knopf, 1994, p. 21.

Chapter 2: The Field of Play

9. Quoted in Burt Solomon, *The Baseball Timeline.* New York: Avon Books, 1997, pp. 3–4.
10. Quoted in John Thorn and Pete Palmer, eds., *Total Baseball.* 3rd ed., New York: HarperPerennial, 1993, p. 2272.
11. Quoted in Thorn and Palmer, *Total Baseball,* p. 2273.
12. Quoted in Thorn and Palmer, *Total Baseball,* p. 2273.
13. Quoted in Thorn and Palmer, *Total Baseball,* p. 2288.
14. Quoted in Chieger, *Voices of Baseball,* p. 173.

Chapter 3: Improving the Game's Image

15. Quoted in Joshua B. Orenstein, "The Union Association of 1884: A Glorious Failure," in *The Baseball Research Journal—1990,* Cleveland, OH: Society for American Baseball Research, 1990, p. 4.
16. Quoted in Cynthia Bass, "The Making

of a Baseball Radical," in *The National Pastime*, Cooperstown, NY: Society for American Baseball Research, 1982, p. 64.

17. Quoted in Chieger, *Voices of Baseball*, p. 103.

18. Quoted in Solomon, *The Baseball Timeline*, p. 102.

19. Quoted in Chieger, *Voices of Baseball*, p. 222.

20. Quoted in Chieger, *Voices of Baseball*, p. 222.

21. Solomon, *The Baseball Timeline*, p. 243.

22. Quoted in Benjamin G. Rader, *Baseball*. Urbana, IL: University of Illinois Press, 1992, pp. 105–106.

23. Quoted in Ward and Burns, *Baseball: An Illustrated History*, p. 179.

Chapter 4: Burning Issues

24. Quoted in Lou Hunsinger Jr., "George W. Stovey," in *The National Pastime–Number 14*, Cleveland, OH: Society for American Baseball Research, 1994, p. 80.

25. Quoted in Bert Randolph Sugar, *Baseball's 50 Greatest Games*. New York: Exeter Books, 1986, p. 132.

26. Quoted in Rader, *Baseball*, p. 150.

27. Quoted in Ward and Burns, *Baseball: An Illustrated History*, p. 276.

28. Quoted in Joe Naiman, "Bert Shepard," in *The National Pastime–Number 19*, Cleveland, OH: Society

for American Baseball Research, 1999, p. 76.

29. Quoted in Chieger, *Voices of Baseball*, p. 121.

30. Quoted in Chieger, *Voices of Baseball*, p. 97.

31. Quoted in Ward and Burns, *Baseball: An Illustrated History*, p. 434.

32. Quoted in Ward and Burns, *Baseball: An Illustrated History*, p. 435.

Chapter 5: The Players Become Empowered

33. Quoted in Rader, *Baseball*, p. 198.

34. Quoted in Solomon, *The Baseball Timeline*, p. 936.

35. Quoted in Phil Pepe and Zander Hollander, *The Baseball Book of Lists*. New York: Pinnacle Books, 1983, p. 181.

36. Quoted in Lee Ivory, "A House Divided," *Baseball Weekly*, July 6–13, 1994, p. 3.

37. Quoted in Pete Williams, "Baseball Finally Finds Some Peace of Mind," *Baseball Weekly*, December 4–10, 1996, p. 6.

38. Quoted in Tim Wendel, "Millionaires: Fans Will Forgive, Forget and Finance," *Baseball Weekly*, April 5–11, 1995, p .6.

39. Quoted in Solomon, *The Baseball Timeline*, p. 1018.

40. Quoted in Hal Bodley, "Selig Sees Game in 'Renaissance,'" *USA Today*,

October 27, 1999, p. 5C.

Chapter 6: The Best of the Best

41. Quoted in Lee Green, ed. *Sportswit.* New York: Fawcett Crest, 1984, p. 22.
42. Quoted in John Holway, ed., *The Sluggers.* Alexandria, VA: Redefinition, 1989, p. 44.
43. Quoted in Mike Shatzkin, ed., *The Ballplayers.* New York: Arbor House, 1990, p. 951.
44. Quoted in Shatzkin, *The Ballplayers,* p. 1.
45. Quoted in Steve Fiffer, *Speed.* Alexandria, VA: Redefinition, 1990, p. 18.
46. Quoted in Chieger, *Voices of Baseball,* p. 138.
47. Quoted in Jim Kaplan, *The Fielders.* Alexandria, VA: Redefinition, 1989, p. 9.
48. Quoted in Kaplan, *The Fielders,* p. 10.
49. Quoted in Pepe and Hollander, *The Baseball Book of Lists,* p. 140.
50. Quoted in Donald Dewey and Nicholas Acocella, *The Biographical History of Baseball.* New York: Carroll and Graf, 1995, p. 447.
51. Quoted in Dewey and Acocella, *The Biographical History of Baseball,* p. 448.

Epilogue: The Year 2000 and Beyond

52. Quoted in Milton Jamail, "Baseball's Latin Market," in *The National Pastime*—Number 12, Cleveland, OH: Society for American Baseball Research, 1992, pp. 84–85.
53. Quoted in Chieger, *Voices of Baseball*, p. 4.

For Further Reading

Books

The Baseball Encyclopedia. New York: Macmillan, 1993. The ninth edition of the famous baseball statistical reference work.

James Charlton, ed., *The Baseball Chronology*. New York: Macmillan, 1991. A day-by-day chronological history of baseball, from 1845 through 1990.

Donald Honig, *The American League*. New York: Crown, 1983. A history of the Junior Circuit, with more than 550 black-and-white photographs.

————, *The National League*. New York: Crown, 1983. A history of the Senior Circuit, with more than 550 black-and-white photographs.

Frederick Ivor-Campbell, Robert L. Tiemann, and Mark Rucker, eds., *Baseball's First Stars*. Cleveland, OH: Society for American Baseball Research, 1996. A second volume of brief biographies of more than 150 early stars of the game.

Daniel Okrent and Harris Lewine, eds., *The Ultimate Baseball Book*. Boston: Houghton Mifflin, 1979. A baseball history, lavishly illustrated with more than eight hundred rare photographs.

Robert L. Tiemann and Mark Rucker, eds., *Nineteenth Century Stars*. Kansas City, MO: Society for American Baseball Research, 1989. Brief biographies of more than 120 early stars of the game.

Websites

Major League Baseball (www.majorleaguebaseball.com). The official website of Major League Baseball contains up-to-the-minute news, as well as articles on baseball history.

National Baseball Hall of Fame (www.baseballhalloffame.org). The official website of the National Baseball Hall of Fame offers information about the Cooperstown shrine.

Total Baseball (www.totalbaseball.com). The on-line version of the invaluable baseball statistical reference.

Works Consulted

Books

Mark Alvarez, *The Old Ball Game*. Alexandria, VA: Redefinition, 1990. This lavishly illustrated volume in the World of Baseball Series gives a detailed look at the early years of the game, up through the 1880s.

Roger Angell, *The Summer Game*. New York: Popular Library, 1972. This is a collection of Angell's pieces which appeared over the years in the *New Yorker*.

The Baseball Research Journal, 1972–1999. Annual publication of the Society for American Baseball Research that presents articles by members writing on history, biography, statistics, and other aspects of baseball.

Jim Bouton, *Ball Four*. New York: Dell, 1971. This is the controversial diary by the former major-league hurler which became the biggest baseball best-seller ever.

Bob Chieger, ed., *Voices of Baseball*. New York: New American Library, 1983. A collection of quotations about baseball topics ranging from baserunning to umpires.

Donald Dewey and Nicholas Acocella, *The Biographical History of Baseball*. New York: Carroll and Graf, 1995. A biographical resource summarizing the contributions of over fifteen hundred players, managers, and executives to the game of baseball.

Steve Fiffer, *Speed*. Alexandria, VA: Redefinition, 1990. Another volume in the World of Baseball Series, this book looks at the various ways in which speed is a factor in the game of baseball.

John Holway, ed., *The Sluggers*. Alexandria, VA: Redefinition, 1989. Another volume in the World of Baseball Series, this book examines the greatest hitters in the game's history.

Ford Hovis, ed., *The Sports Encyclopedia*. New York: Rutledge Books, 1976. This book contains a description of every modern-day sport. Included are sections on history, equipment, strategy, and scoring.

Bill James, *The Bill James Historical Baseball Abstract*. New York: Villard Books, 1986. A historical analysis of the game as seen through the eyes of one of the game's foremost analysts.

Jim Kaplan, *The Fielders*. Alexandria, VA: Redefinition, 1989. Another volume in the World of Baseball Series, this book takes a look at the often overlooked art of fielding.

Justin Kaplan, ed., *Bartlett's Familiar Quotations*. 16th ed. Boston: Little, Brown, 1992. Contains many famous quotations, including a selection from baseball.

Phil Pepe and Zander Hollander, *The Baseball Book of Lists*. New York: Pinnacle Books, 1983. A compilation of 174 baseball lists, ranging from the All-Hollywood Baseball Team to Things Certain to Happen During a Baseball Rain Delay.

Benjamin G. Rader, *Baseball*. Urbana, IL: University of Illinois Press, 1992. This volume in the Illinois History of Sports Series examines the history of the game and how it helped shape American society.

The National Pastime, Cooperstown, NY: Society for American Baseball Research, 1982–1999. Collections of articles published annually by the Society for American Baseball Research.

Neil Schlager, ed., *How Products Are Made*. Detroit, MI: Gale Research, 1994. This voluminous book describes how many everyday objects are manufactured.

Mike Shatzkin, ed., *The Ballplayers*. New York: Arbor House, 1990. The ultimate baseball biographical reference, containing over five thousand biographies.

Burt Solomon, *The Baseball Timeline*. New York: Avon Books, 1997. A comprehensive day-by-day history of baseball from 1778 to 1996.

Bert Randolph Sugar, *Baseball's 50 Greatest Games*. New York: Exeter Books, 1986. A detailed examination of the fifty greatest games of all time and the events leading up to them.

John Thorn and Pete Palmer, eds., *Total Baseball*. 3rd ed., New York: Harper-Perennial, 1993. A comprehensive baseball reference, containing statistics and historical essays.

Geoffrey C. Ward and Ken Burns, *Baseball: An Illustrated History*. New York: Alfred A. Knopf, 1994. A beautifully illustrated history of the national pastime to accompany the television series.

Periodicals

Hal Bodley, "Selig Sees Game in 'Renaissance,'" *USA Today*, October 27, 1999.

Lee Ivory, "A House Divided," *Baseball Weekly*, July 6–13, 1994.

Bill Madden, "Safe at Home," *New York Daily News*, May 17, 1998.

Tim Wendel, "Millionaires: Fans Will Forgive, Forget and Finance," *Baseball Weekly*, April 5–11, 1995.

Pete Williams, "Baseball Finally Finds Some Peace of Mind," *Baseball Weekly*, December 4–10, 1996.

Index

Picture Credits

Cover photo: © Jack Zehrt/FPG International
© AFP/Corbis, 8
AP Photo/Rob Burns, 60
AP Photo/Harry Harris, 31
AP Photo/Ted Matthias, 64
AP Photo/Mike Pettit, 72
Archive Photos, 12, 68
© Bettmann/Corbis, 19, 38, 52, 69, 74, 75, 82
Blank Archives/Archive Photos, 43
© Jim Cummins/FPG International, 26
© Henry Diltz/Corbis, 54
© FPG International, 35
© Keystone Pictures Inc./FPG International, 48
© Paul Thompson Photos/FPG International, 41
Photo File/Archive Photos, 29, 39
© Photoworld/FPG International, 11
© Neal Preston/Corbis, 78
© Reuters/Gary Brady/Archive Photos, 71
© Reuters Newmedia Inc/Corbis, 23
© Reuters/Blake Sell/Archive Photos, 65
© Paul A. Souders/Corbis, 13
Sporting News/Archive Photos, 45, 49
Morton Tadder/Archive Photos, 55
© Underwood & Underwood/Corbis, 61

About the Author

John F. Grabowski is a native of Brooklyn, New York. He holds a bachelor's degree in psychology from City College of New York and a master's degree in educational psychology from Teacher's College, Columbia University. He has been a teacher for thirty-one years, as well as a freelance writer, specializing in the fields of sports, education, and comedy. His body of published work includes twenty-two books; a nationally syndicated sports column; consultation on several math textbooks; articles for newspapers, magazines, and the programs of professional sports teams; and comedy material sold to Jay Leno, Joan Rivers, and numerous other comics. He and his wife, Patricia, live in Staten Island with their daughter, Elizabeth.

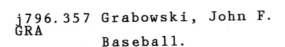